Love, Fate and Afghanistan

Tony Thomson

To a fellow dog
walker

Tony

ISBN: 1452870322
ISBN-13: 9781452870328

For Our Children

CONTENTS

Love, Fate, and Afghanistan is a memoir, not a work of history. Facts and dates have been checked to the best of my ability. A few names have been changed for reasons that will be obvious.

Eastern Roads: 1971

In Nepal: Tony and Alyson when Young and Crazy

Q. How Do You Drive from London to India?

A. Turn Left at Istanbul.

Q. Why Drive from London to India?

A. To Find Your Heart's Desire.

.

I am a midwestern American, Cincinnati born and Cleveland raised. In January 1971, aged twenty-seven, I was working in London for Kleinwort Benson, a traditional British merchant bank. I'd been there since coming down from Oxford in 1969. I hadn't planned to stay in England after going to Oxford on the GI Bill, but England in the late sixties and early seventies throbbed with wild music and sneering, disrespectful humor. Life was fun! I planned to sample everything before leaving. Especially the girls.

I went to Oxford after three years in the US Army, including a year in Vietnam, then a year to finish up at Yale. At Keble, my college at Oxford, working hard academically was neither required nor customary. I worked spasmodically in the college library but spent more time rowing in an eight on the Thames. Weekends I went up to London or went to stay with my English cousins, the Kershaws, in Gloucestershire.

The head of the family, Sir Anthony Kershaw MC MP, was actually only my distant cousin, but Anthony and his wife, Barbara, were the parents I would have chosen in a perfect world. After a heroic World War II spent as a tank officer fighting Rommel in the desert, Anthony became a Member of Parliament. Anthony knew about everything that was going on in the world.

Barbara was shrewd and fun. She teased me into eating things like oysters and puff balls fried in butter and garlic that boys from Ohio didn't eat. The Kershaws tried to open the wacky world of upper-crust English society to me. I was socially too awkward to take full advantage of their efforts, but the eccentric people I met through them made me appreciate the social accuracy of Evelyn Waugh and P.G. Wodehouse.

Some years before, I'd turned up one summer in England as a tall, skinny, gauche teenager. Barbara promptly sent me off to travel rough in Greece with her son, Harry, my taller and larger but much less gauche contemporary.

Travel with Harry, along with my time as an inmate of a traditional New England boarding school, prepared me brilliantly for the army and for any form of uncomfortable traveling. We tried everything.

We woke up with splitting hangovers after sleeping under olive trees and endured agonizing gut rot from eating in the cheapest and dirtiest Greek restaurants. We travelled on scooters, mostly helmetless and often drunkenly.

At Oxford, I spent most of my time fooling around with my South African Rhodes Scholar pal, Tudor Caradoc Davies. In the 1970s, many young Brits, especially university students, had Vietnam-related hang-ups about Americans. White South Africans were even more suspect. Tudor gave up his beloved rugby after having his nose broken repeatedly by kicks and elbows in the face during scrums.

British undergraduates lumped all English-speaking non-Brits together. At best we were distastefully peculiar. At worst we were colonialist and capitalist and thus a sure source of moral contamination. We found this attitude droll. We were older than the British undergraduates, and so were assigned to a different student common room along with the geeky British PhD students. Tudor and I stuck together as outsiders. Eventually, Tudor's delightful girlfriend, Gill, who was already a medical doctor, joined him. In due course I was best man at their wedding.

Tudor had found his mate, but I was still spare.

In most other ways, my life was a hoot, but what I craved was a real live English girlfriend.

England was a pleasure dome. To share these pleasures with a beautiful English girl was my heart's desire. English girls were lovely. They had beautiful skin and long, soft hair. They laughed at jokes, even mine. They made puns!

Best of all, English girls weren't in the least like my mother or all the other bossy, boring, suburban American women and girls I knew, with voices like sea gulls fighting over a dead fish.

English girls wore ridiculously short skirts and pink lipstick. They shouted obscenities and drank themselves silly. They liked sex and said so out loud.

After finishing Oxford, I decided to stay in England for a while. Having no qualifications other than history degrees from Yale and Oxford and no skills other than those of a former artilleryman in the US Army, I was unsure how to find a job. Plus, as an American, I would need my employer to obtain a British work permit for me.

In an inspired moment, I asked Bobby, the husband of one of my English cousins, if he knew of a suitable job in the City—the London financial district where Bobby worked as a director of a merchant bank. To my amazement, Bobby immediately suggested that I join his bank as a financial analyst in their stock market research department.

"Great, I'm your man," I said. "What is a financial analyst?"

So, I busied myself at Kleinworts for several years. In those long-ago days, Kleinworts, like the other, now-vanished London merchant banks, was a small, cozy partnership controlled by the Kleinwort family. It employed a few hundred people.

I was the only American employee of Kleinworts and so was frequently questioned about the US economy, about which I knew nothing. Or I was questioned about American business methods, about which I knew even less.

Through carefully reading the *Financial Times* every morning, I soon learned how to make up suitable replies. For the worried, I suggested that US inflation might go up next year. For the optimists, I opined that the US stock market outlook wasn't so bad. For those interested in US business methods, I quoted the famous American management guru Peter Drucker, whose shrewd comments featured in many *FT* articles and whose books I have still never read a word of.

I made large charts of economic trends. My favorite was my massive chart of the hog cycle. The hog cycle chart traced the number of sows that were slaughtered. If too many sows were turned into pork chops, there would be fewer piglets, and eventually the price of pig meat would raise—good news for one of Kleinwort's investments. I rediscovered how incompetent I was in doing math calculations using a slide rule, but generally the work was interesting. I also made several lifelong friends.

One day, I discovered that our young, pretty team assistant was paid much more than I was. When I questioned Don, the head of research, about this obvious mistake, that jovial man said in unfeigned astonishment, "But Sue is valuable."

———◆———

Time passed pleasantly enough. In the evenings there were Suzy, Jeannie, and later Serena. There was pub theatre in little smoky rooms above The Fox and the Ferret and big time theatre, like the original *Hair*, in London's west end. Dinner for two with wine at my sort of restaurant cost five pounds, or a bit more than ten dollars. London in the early 1970s also offered many less-conventional pleasures carried over from the mad, rocking sixties.

Somehow, though, I longed for something more that I had no name for. Action was required and now! But what action?

Hearing that Angkor Wat was destroyed gave me an awful jolt. The ever-expanding Vietnam War had spilled over into Cambodia. In fact, Angkor Wat was undamaged. This was only a peacenik antiwar rumor, but at the time I believed it and felt completely cheated. I had always dreamed of going to Angkor Wat after reading about it in *National Geographic* as a child.

In this mood, I met the Honourable Jane Ashley at a drinks party.

As the daughter of a British earl, Jane was an "Honourable," but in person she was more like a member of a Californian hippie commune than like a traditional upper-class English debutante. Or indeed like a traditional anything. Jane defecated on all traditions.

A few years younger than I was, the Honourable Jane was small breasted and slender, with prominent cheekbones and irregular, tobacco-stained teeth. Jane had short, dark brown hair cut in a boyish style, drank little but smoked unfiltered French Gauloise cigarettes continuously, lighting a fresh one from the previous gummy, smoldering butt. Jane never wore anything to parties (or to anywhere else) but a T-shirt and worn, grubby jeans. Lipstick was her only party concession.

Jane was attractive in a gamine way, very bright, and verbally quick. We had nothing, but nothing, in common. At the drinks party, we were thrown together by our mutual shyness and by our complete lack of interest in the other drinkers' chatter.

Jane had already crossed Turkey and Iran by bus and had travelled rough in India. She wanted to make another expedition.

"Why don't we drive from London to India?" suggested Jane. "My God, no one should work in a bank! You need to find yourself! It may not be too late!"

Jane sketched a vivid picture of driving through high passes; of meeting strange, inscrutable tribal people; of listening to spiritually uplifting saffron-robed gurus; and of spending time in incense-filled ashrams. Wow! This could be better than the flower-power scene in California that I'd missed by joining the army in 1963.

As we parted, Jane ordered me to read *The Wilder Shores of Love* by Lesley Blanch at once.

During my lunch break the next day, I found a used copy of *The Wilder Shores of Love* in a little bookshop in the Charing Cross Road. This remarkable and unjustly forgotten book tells the history of four brave, adventurous Western women who find sex, romance, and varying degrees of happiness in the East. The illustrations in the book are of dervishes and the harem. The stories include that of the real woman whose life was the basis of Mozart's great opera, *The Abduction from the Seraglio*. These women suffered, yes, but they lived life to the fullest.

Jane and Lesley Blanch had hooked me. The East beckoned. Follow your star; that was the thing.

And this was not sex; Jane and I were, then and always, platonic soul mates—not even true friends. I also quickly realized that in addition to being adventurous and romantic, Jane was desperately screwed up in some seriously complicated, female English way that was completely outside my experience. No matter.

Jane and I met sporadically over the next few weeks. Her overland travels in the East had mostly been on local public buses, leaving her utterly fed up with bus travel. The true, spiritual hippies were fun, but the other Western bus travelers were smelly, unpleasant, and druggy. The buses stopped in dismal, boring places. You had to sleep in flea pits.

"Why don't we"—meaning me—"buy a VW Bus and drive ourselves?" asked Jane.

Jane had a girlfriend who would come along for at least part of the way. And the girlfriend knew a young English ex-army officer who would join us if asked. We would carry others for a fee. The cost to me would be little more than the cost of a used VW Bus. Nothing really.

At this point I did one sensible thing. I went to WH Smith, the British news agents, and bought two red cloth-covered notebooks, which I still have. I felt the need to record what I was doing. I also needed a place to make lists and doodle. I knew that I was doing something mold-breaking and wanted a record of it.

However, even after rereading the red journals, it is hard for me to understand my thinking and my actions then.

Such feeble reasoning as I bothered with went something like this: my young adult life had been spent in the US Army and at universities. The earth-shaking 1960s had rushed past me before I'd even had the opportunity not to inhale. Boredom was my mortal enemy but boredom in large chunks looked more and more like my future. Avanti! Carpe diem!

It was February. There was no question of our leaving until early summer since we planned to camp out all the way to India. Nonetheless, I promptly informed Kleinworts that I would be leaving at the end of my one-month notice period. Kleinworts humored me by suggesting that I take an unpaid leave of absence, though with no guarantee that I would get my job back.

"That will not be necessary," said I, though I wasn't sure I even had enough money to cover the cost of the trip.

Obviously, a great deal of planning was needed for such a challenging trip. Naturally, I decided instead to go immediately to

Austria in order to learn how to ski competently. I spent the next month in St. Anton in the Austrian Arlberg, which then had the best ski school in the world. With a lot of work and the help of a patient but demanding ski Lehrer, by the end of the month I could ski awkwardly, unstylishly, but on any sort of slope, even on the huge moguls—bumps—on Gampen and Galzig above St. Anton.

While wondering what to do next, a Scottish skiing pal with the wonderful name of Henrietta Ogilvie-Wedderburn asked me to drive her from St. Anton over to Verbier, a Swiss ski resort. She was joining a large ski chalet party, organized by a guy who lusted after her. I knew a chalet in Verbier where I could stay cheaply, so I said okay without a thought.

Kismet…

Enter Alyson

We arrived in Verbier in a driving snow storm. I dropped Henrietta off at her chalet, parked, and offloaded my stuff at my chalet, and wandered back to see what kind of a party Henrietta had joined. Verbier is a purpose-built, modern ski resort, full of traditional-looking but ersatz Swiss chalets, complete with stained wooden shutters, low-pitched tiled roofs, and lots of large, rough stones inside and out. Only the cows were missing.

The whole of a very British chalet party was milling around in the snowy yard in front of their large, white-stucco chalet. An assortment of ropey-looking rental skis was dumped on the snow in front of the chalet. The would-be skiers were matching them to their rental boots. (This is not a smart way to select rental skis, as Alyson would soon find out.)

By now, the snow was falling harder and faster. The tops of the mountains were lost in a total whiteout. Big flakes of wet snow fell on my face when I looked up to where the mountains should be.

I suggested to several people that they give skiing a miss for the afternoon and join me for a boozy lunch, but all the Brits, save one, were anxious to hit the slopes. The one was a girl in brown ill-fitting ski pants, a brown-and-blue spotted anorak and a brown, loose-knitted wooly hat. She was tall and slender but shapely. Two enormous blue eyes peeked out from under the brown woolly hat, as did some strands of long, lustrous, brunette hair. Her name was Alyson Vero, she said, and she would love to have lunch with me. Apart from her unfortunate color scheme, Alyson was simply gorgeous. (The clothes were on loan from an older sister.)

Alyson and I had a cheese fondue for lunch in a small, dark cave of a restaurant, and then talked all afternoon over many pitchers of Fendant, the local Swiss white wine. Like me, Alyson was also on the cusp of doing something completely different with her life. One of five daughters, she was born into a huntin', shootin', fishin' county family in Leicestershire in the English Midlands.

Blocked by her father from going to university, Alyson left home and went up to London at seventeen, where she thrived, becoming the personal assistant to one of London's major theatrical producers.

I knew many bright English girls who were thwarted in their desire to go to university like their male peers. English fathers in the 1960s regarded university education for their daughters in the same way they regarded automatic transmissions for their cars: unnecessary, expensive, and wasteful.

Most bright, classy English girls, faced with this patriarchal diktat, passively accepted roles as secretaries at publishing houses or as sales assistants in art galleries while waiting for marriage to rescue them. The small talk of these girls tended to focus on the sexual peculiarities of people in their circle and on parties, horse racing, and dogs.

Not Alyson. She fiercely resented not going to university. She disliked her Midlands background, her father's sexism, and the apathy of her female peers. She wanted adventure and a challenging life. Alyson loved working in the theatre, but she was about to quit her job and move to Italy to study art and learn Italian.

Pukka English girls in those days didn't talk about themselves or about anything that actually mattered.

In total contrast, Alyson was joltingly frank and open about everything. She asked probing questions about who I was and about what I was doing; about what I thought and about what I felt.

If I answered her flippantly or, as was my habit then, replied with some quote from G. K. Chesterton or Oscar Wilde that I thought clever, Alyson would tip her head slightly to one side and look at me in silence. With her huge blue eyes, the effect on me was discomforting; what a mouse must feel when it realizes that an owl in the tree above is watching its every move.

After hours of talking, we arranged to go dancing after dinner that evening. And that evening, while dancing, we arranged to go skiing the following morning. That Alyson had never skied before and that my ski teaching qualifications were nonexistent, we ignored.

The next morning I overslept. So did Alyson. By the time I walked down to her chalet, I found that Alyson had kitted up and gone off to ski with a male member of her party. I'd missed her by minutes. No matter, I'd catch up with her at the mountain restaurant at Les Ruinettes where everyone ate.

I went up to the top of the series of lifts and skied down to the restaurant. So there I was, sitting in the sun on the terrace at Les Ruinettes, enjoying a glass of red wine and a plate of frites—the only remotely affordable things on the menu—chatting away with Henrietta and her chalet party when there was a loud female shout of "oy" from a passing "blood wagon." The blood wagon, a sled with one rescue guy on skis at the back and another at the front, is used to carry injured skiers down the mountain.

Blood wagons made their way down the mountain with disturbing frequency. Undamaged skiers tried to ignore them. But this one would not be ignored. The shouting body on the blood wagon threw the cover off, told the two Swiss guys who were piloting the device to hold on for a moment, and limped over to the terrace, demanded a glass of wine, and asked me, "Where the hell were you this morning? See what you made me do!"

It was, of course, Alyson, who had just shattered her left ankle through being led off into some deep snow by her amorous, amateur ski teacher. In the deep snow, Alyson achieved a spiral fracture through pivoting on the cheap rental skis whose rusty safety bindings didn't release.

Though this definitely wrecked any plans that the other would-be ski teacher may have had for fun with Alyson, it didn't seem to have done me any good either. Through some quirk of the female mind, Alyson then and later held me one hundred percent responsible for her broken ankle, though we both had overslept and so missed our meeting. I wasn't even present at the scene of the accident, for heaven's sake.

Deciding that this was no time to argue the facts of the case, I and others helped her back into the blood wagon after she glugged down a glass of wine. We saw her off down the mountain, with one sturdy Swiss snow-plowing at the front of the blood wagon and another one at the back.

That evening, I popped into the clinic that held a monopoly on health care in Verbier. The clinic was owned and run by Dr. Jesus Filletti, an entrepreneurial, completely Swiss doctor despite his un-Swiss name.

Dr. Jesus roamed the clinic wearing felt clogs, black trousers, and a blood-stained grey turtleneck while carrying a brandy bottle in one hand and a large cigar in the other. Dr. Jesus didn't drink the brandy; it was for patients and their worried friends and relatives. Apart from the cigar, the rest of the outfit was his operating-room kit. Offering me a shot of cognac, the doctor told me that Alyson had her ankle surgically pinned, that the result was a surgical masterpiece, and that she wanted to see me.

Only Dr. Jesus' first statement turned out to be more-or-less accurate.

Alyson was groggy with anesthetic and didn't want to see anyone. The next day she was evacuated to London, where it quickly became apparent that Dr. Jesus had botched the work on her ankle and completely missed an injury to her knee. Within days, we got word that she would need another operation to reset the ankle.

When I went back to the clinic and asked the good doctor why he had left Alyson in such a mess, he cheerfully claimed that his success rate was high but that any doctor who did as many ankle operations as he did was bound to have the occasional off day. Dr. Jesus was such a charmer that it was hard to be annoyed with him. Plus he gave me another belt of excellent cognac. And after all, it wasn't my ankle.

But I did feel badly about Alyson's accident. Had I failed this wonderful, beautiful girl? As soon as I returned to London, I went to see Alyson. She'd had her ankle operation and was in the Italian Hospital in Queen's Square. So off I went to the Italian Hospital, buying a bunch of violets on the way.

In those days, real live nuns wearing habits were the nurses at the Italian Hospital. (Since then the Italian Hospital has been replaced by a block of luxury flats, and nursing nuns are history in the developed world.) But then the nuns were led by a splendid senior sister who was indeed Italian, very sweet, not too old, and had an artificial leg. (Alyson told me this, but I might have guessed it from the noise the sister made as she walked.)

This sister greeted me warmly with a big Italian smile. Without asking Alyson, Sister Maria said that Alyson would be delighted to see me and told me to go right into Alyson's hospital room. And she asked if I wanted milk or sugar in my coffee.

Alyson was indeed pleased to see me since, with her leg in the air, she was going mad with boredom and from the itching under her plaster cast. And she loved the little bunch of violets I brought. After she forcefully reminded me at length of my failure, Alyson and I lapsed back into the probing-but-fun chit chat about ourselves that we had started in the fondue restaurant. I was greatly distracted by her loose, wonderful, thick, dark brunette hair against the pillows and by occasional glimpses of her small, firm breasts but managed somehow to keep up my end of the conversation.

Time passed swimmingly.

Sister Maria popped in with a tray of sandwiches, then later with afternoon tea. Much later, she returned unasked with a scotch and soda for me and a glass of Chianti for Alyson. Looking out the window, I noticed that it was dark. I was ready to stay the night and talk until daybreak, but Alyson said emphatically that she was tired. (Later Alyson told me that she had actually desperately wanted a pee.)

As I walked down the corridor to leave, I noticed Sister Maria talking with a couple of younger nuns in a side room. They all turned to look at me in a friendly but scrutinizing way. One nun called down the corridor after me as I passed their room and told me to come back whenever I wanted. What a wonderful hospital, I thought, and what caring nuns. No rules and no visiting hours. It was only later that I realized that the nuns, however devoted to nursing and to their Church, were still true Italian women and saw a budding romance that they should encourage. Matchmaking was dear to their gentle hearts.

By the time Alyson left the Italian Hospital, I was gobsmacked by her. Was she the One? Was I in love? If so, why was I afraid of her? Could she peer into my very soul with those huge, beautiful eyes? Was something happening to me against my will? Why did Alyson look at me as though I were insane when I proudly told her that I could fit all my possessions into a London taxi? Why did she talk about wanting to own a London house? We were free; why would we want to be tied down?

I gave Alyson my copy of *The Wilder Shores of Love*. Alyson loved it as much as I did. This was a good sign. For me, loving this enchanting book was proof that a woman had a romantic imagination and an adventurous spirit.

It was now spring in London, that time of golden daffodils in the parks, best glimpsed through a taxi window due to the cold, constant drizzle.

When Alyson finally got the cast off her ankle, I suggested that we go somewhere warm. Without hesitation, Alyson said that a trip was a perfectly wonderful idea and that she had always wanted to see Venice, just as I suggested. Not having had any destination in mind financially further away than the south coast of England, I mumbled that this was a perfect plan and rushed off to buy the cheapest air tickets to Venice I could find. When Alyson asked where we would stay, I explained patiently that the secret of real travel was simply to arrive and see what beckoned. She took this imbecile nonsense surprisingly well.

After a crowded and uncomfortable flight, we arrived at the vaporetto (water bus) terminal in Venice. Once there, the question of which hotel to choose could not be ducked.

Alyson was used to masterful men who booked luxurious hotels in advance and who knew all the good restaurants. She did not want to be consulted about such details. Grasping at straws, I noticed an ad for a Hotel la Fenice and remembered that Alyson wanted to visit the Theatro la Fenice. This hotel was next to the theatro, the ad said. And so, off to the Hotel la Fenice we went.

After the boat dropped us in old Venice, the walk to the hotel was fun but a bit of a struggle.

This was the first time I'd travelled anywhere with a gorgeous woman. It was also the first time I'd travelled with a woman who took clothes and makeup for any possible situation along with her entire collection of pet rocks in an immensely heavy, old cloth-and-leather suitcase covered with stickers from the Mauretania and Le Train Bleu.

The afternoon was beautiful, blue of sky and fleecy of cloud. Sweat poured off me as we crossed short, high-humped bridges and skirted narrow canals. Alyson was beaming with pleasure. I was thrilled to be with her. Along the way, Alyson bought two kilos (4.4 pounds) of beautiful, ripe cherries. I wondered how and when we would eat so many cherries but was told that the plan was to take them back to England for fruit-loving friends.

From the outside, the Hotel la Fenice looked quaint—a grey, ancient, flat-fronted building of a few stories and floor-to-ceiling shutter-framed windows. The hotel was indeed just to the side of the famous theatro. Our problems began when we went in. Did the signori have a reservation? The hotel was quite full. Alyson smiled at the room clerk, and a room facing the theatre was found to be free after all. We went up the creaking stairs with the manager groaning behind us, carrying Alyson's suitcase. With hindsight, I should have tipped him more generously.

The room seemed perfect; it was complete with a view of the theatre. True, the single bed appeared designed for a solitary Italian of traditional Latin physique; it was narrow, soft and short. We were two tall Anglo-Saxons, but no matter; we would be joined as one in it. Love would find a way.

After unpacking everything from many books about Venice to her electric hair dryer, Alyson carefully washed the cherries. Even in those ignorant, long ago days prior to the organic revelation, we knew that it was important not to allow vile chemicals into our bodies. Plus the cherries needed to be dry for the trip back. So Alyson rolled them up carefully in a clean hotel towel to dry on the floor under the open window. Wrapped in the towel, the cherries formed a lump about the size and shape of a section of drain pipe.

We wandered about Venice aimlessly for a bit, then had a simple meal in a tourist trattoria. The wine was like the blood of an alcoholic ox and the veal like leather, but we were happy. Under a waxing moon, we made our way back to the hotel, hugging and kissing to the approval of the passers-by. After quick showers, we settled in for our first night together.

The night, alas, was not a huge success from my perspective or from Alyson's. Much light and continual noisy shouting came in through the large window. The room was sweltering. Smells from ancient drains tainted the air. The deep U-shape of the mattress complicated my fumbling efforts as a lover. Alyson was patient and passionate, but basically I was afraid of her. After some compensatory cuddling, we agreed that we were tired, very tired. And hot, very hot. We kicked off everything but the sheet.

We tried lying back to back and side by side, then on our stomachs. The bed was so short that Alyson's feet were against the foot board. I had to keep my knees bent. Sleep came and went—mostly went—in fitful snatches. I managed to elbow Alyson in the nose at one point. Perhaps accidentally, she managed to kick me hard somewhat later. And there were mosquitoes.

This was the kind of night that we came to call a "night of bliss." Morning arrived as a great relief.

"Shall we get up," I asked?

"Is there an alternative?" Alyson replied.

I sprang from the bed and rushed to the window for a reviving view of La Fenice and some air.

It was just bad luck that I managed to plant both of my size-twelve feet on the towel full of cherries, then stomp around on them. Cherry juice went everywhere; the cherries were indeed perfectly ripe. The juice stained the towel and the carpet; it ran all over the floor.

Using the only other towel in the room, we managed to get a lot of the juice off the floor and off the carpet but only by ruining the other towel as well. We flushed most of the cherries down the loo without actually blocking it, which was fortunate, but we did completely stain the loo bowl and the loo seat an indelible bright red. There were also brilliant red cherry-juice handprints on the bed and around the washbasin.

If Sultan Mahomet the Magnificent had deflowered his full harem of Circassian virgins in one passionate night, and the next morning told Abdul, the chief eunuch, to clean up the bloody results with a pitcher of water and a handkerchief, you might obtain the same effect. The room could have been the setting of an ax murder. It screamed for a tourniquet.

We sat on the edge of the horrid, sagging bed and looked at each other.

"What do we do?" said Alyson.

"Go have a quick breakfast, then check out fast," I said. "I can't handle this without coffee. With luck, we can check out before the chambermaid comes on duty."

Breakfast was okay, I suppose, though conversation didn't flow. We slunk back into the Hotel Fenice, packed like lightning, and checked out. But our haggard, furtive look inspired the manager to buzz the chambermaid to go and ensure that we hadn't stolen the bidet.

The result was that, just as I passed through the hotel's front door and into the street with Alyson's monster suitcase, there was the most awful screaming and cursing in Italian from the window of our room. A big, fat, enraged woman was leaning out yelling, "Basta! Lei e' un cafone strongo!" I accelerated, and Alyson ran ahead.

We got away.

As an antidote, we checked into an excellent hotel. For the rest of the day, we planned to do the things lovers did in Venice. We went in a gondola. We admired Santa Maria del Salute. We sat in the pews of the Church of the Friari. At that point we felt the need for a drink and had one in St. Mark's Square. The next step was to go into St Mark's.

Wandering through this ancient and magnificent church, full of the treasures that the Venetians had bought or stolen from all over the Mediterranean world, we were drawn upwards in the building. Hand-in-hand, we found our way onto the balcony where the four famous horses overlook St. Mark's Square. Taken by the beauty of the scene and the reigniting of our passion, we locked in a lusty embrace. At that point, an aged, uniformed Catholic beadle stepped out from behind one of the horses and gave us our second "basta!" of the day. We were thrown out of St. Mark's and told not to return.

Neither of us was sorry to leave Venice.

Back in London, I realized that prompt action was needed if our expedition was to set off in the direction of India any time soon. The Honourable Jane and I worked out a list of things that we thought we would need. A VW Bus headed the list, so I went far out London's Edgeware Road to where the proper car dealers gave way to used car dealers with names like Honest Syd, and the car prices were marked in easy-to-rub-off white paint on the inside of the cars' windscreens.

I had expected lengthy haggling to buy a decent VW Bus but immediately found one at a sensible price that was in excellent condition. Elsie, or ELC 954, had left-hand drive so she didn't suit the British market but was perfect for what I had in mind. Elsie was probably a 1968 model since, unlike the old California surfers' delight, Elsie had a one-piece windscreen and a slightly larger engine with about fifty throbbing horsepower. The rear engine was the familiar VW flat four, air-cooled design, created by Dr. Porsche for his pal, Adolf Hitler. Mechanically, Elsie was bog standard apart from having an oversized air cleaner.

I'd worked on friends' VW Beetles. They were so ingeniously simple that there wasn't much to go wrong. After a brief test drive, I felt comfortable that Elsie was more-or-less okay mechanically, so I bought her on the spot.

Over the next week, I cleaned the air cleaner by washing the wire-mesh air filter in gasoline. I put in four new spark plugs and bought an extra rotor arm for the distributor and a couple of spare headlight bulbs. Finally I had four London taxi tires fitted. These were old-fashioned cross-ply tires, not radial-ply, with a thick pad of rubber on the outer side of the tires' sidewalls. The thick rubber pad was to prevent damage if the taxi hit a curb or rock. Cross-ply tires are easy to repair, plus they had inner tubes as a second line of defense against flats.

Those were my sole mechanical preparations for the trip. I was immediately told by everyone I talked to that we would encounter mechanical disaster. A VW Bus was totally inadequate for such an arduous drive. A Land Rover or a four-wheel-drive surplus British army truck was the thing. During the long drive, therefore, it was always a pleasure to drive past broken-down Land Rovers and ex-British army trucks, of which we saw quite a few.

Jane was working on supplies. I paid little attention to this, though it was clear from the start that her idea of our requirements was eccentric. She bought a huge amount of Nescafe instant coffee and boxes and boxes of Typhoo teabags, along with enough sugar and powdered skim milk for an infantry company. The tea and coffee were presumably to be used to wash down the equally large amounts of Knorr powdered soups Jane bought. To boil water and heat the soups, Jane bought a Camping Gaz stove that perched on top of a small, blue, gas canister. So she also bought several boxes of twenty gas canisters each, along with two Camping Gaz mantle lights that similarly screwed into the gas cylinders.

To round out our diet, Jane added many, many packs of instant noodles. A few pans, a jerry can for water, and a large amount of liquid detergent completed Jane's housekeeping stores.

I bought a cheap but large tent that was easy to erect, plus a few old British Army surplus camp beds. These beds consisted of a rectangular piece of canvas that stretched with nail-breaking difficulty over a collapsible metal frame. I also bought five surplus sleeping bags that weren't too obviously filthy. It seemed wise to have a spare sleeping bag. I remembered some unpleasant sleeping bag user mishaps during army training exercises. I loaded all of this kit any old way into empty cardboard boxes from a local convenience store.

At this point we were only a few weeks away from our hypothetical departure date. Someone reminded me that we would need visas for almost every country we would drive through, so Jane and I rushed around to various consulates and left our passports overnight, along with what seemed then a large amount of money, to obtain the necessary visa stamps.

Jane took my US passport along with her UK one to the Iranian consulate so they were processed together. When I got my passport back, I looked at the pretty visa stamp with strange Persian numerals handwritten on it but thought no further about it. This Iranian visa later proved to be the source of a particularly irritating problem.

Jane also realized that it was time to involve her friend, Shelby, who was to go with us, plus the so-far nebulous ex-army officer. Accordingly, Jane, Shelby, and I met in a pub.

The meeting was an awkward one. Shelby McGrath was about the same age as Jane but a university graduate who'd had a series of entry-level managerial jobs. Shelby was Northern Irish middle class and had all the pugnacity for which Ulster folk are known. (The American Generals Grant, Sherman, Sheridan, and MacArthur were all of Northern Irish Protestant stock.)

Shelby was a good-looking, athletic blonde. Initially, she wasn't exactly unfriendly but certainly sharp and aggressive. It wasn't clear how she knew Jane. This didn't come out during the conversation, and for some reason I didn't ask. They certainly had nothing in common. I wondered briefly if something sapphic was involved but quickly dropped the idea. Both had a lively interest in men, though not in me fortunately.

My goal for the pub meeting was to plan the trip. Shelby's goal was to kick my tires thoroughly, though she always claimed to like Americans in general. (It was individual Americans that she had problems with.) This launched us badly, a trend that would continue.

The next day, Jane and I met with the ex-officer. Normally, I can remember names and even scraps of conversations decades afterwards. This guy was such a complete twit and such a perfect caricature of a type of tall, gawky, upper-class Brit that he made no impression on me whatsoever. Let's call him Julian.

I remember that Julian mumbled a bit about being glad to come along but otherwise didn't offer to help in any way with getting ready. It wasn't clear whether he was a friend of Jane's or of Shelby's or why they had picked him. I decided that this didn't matter as along as he paid his way. The theory was that I would pay for the vehicle but that we would divide equally all other expenses.

Another final step was to obtain an old-fashioned customs document, called a carnet, for India. To bring a vehicle into India meant that you needed a third party such as a bank to guarantee financially that you would take it out again.

Everything to do with foreign-made autos, from an actual auto to spare auto parts, was absurdly expensive in India at that time. Clinging to the regulation-mad, bureaucratic socialism that they had picked up at the London School of Economics, the Indian political elite were attempting to create a new, autarchic, socialist India behind high-tariff walls. Creating a one hundred percent Indian domestic auto industry was part of the project. That such an approach offered immense opportunities for bribery and corruption was no doubt part of its local appeal, though it also attracted much approval from European left wing commentators.

To my utter amazement, Barclays Bank issued me with a carnet without any fuss and for only a small fee. Things seemed too easy.

At this point I talked to Anthony Kershaw about the trip. Anthony thought that the trip was a great idea but added that no matter how carefully we planned—which we certainly had not—we would encounter difficulties. Flexibility was the thing! Rommel had taught the British Army to be flexible.

Flexibility was the essence of driving across barren lands and deserts, even if Rommel wasn't around to complicate matters. There was, however, one item that was so essential that we must not leave without one. This object had saved Anthony untold misery during the desert campaign.

"Dear boy," said Anthony, "You mustn't leave without a thunderbox. Desert life without one is unbearable."

With a little research, a thunderbox, or kharzi, was located in an army surplus store near Victoria Station. It consisted of a square wooden seat with an oval hole of suitable size for an adult human bottom with four detachable wooden legs, each leg being connected to the seat by a stout cord. It wouldn't do to find a leg missing on some gloomy night in a dry wadi. With the legs detached, the thunderbox fit neatly into a robust British Army khaki canvas case with a carrying handle.

At the urging of the store clerk, I also bought a British Army surplus entrenching tool. The entrenching tool is a small shovel with a hinged shaft. The shovel blade folds flat against the shaft so that the entrenching tool fits into a canvas case that hangs on a webbing belt or pack. Suitably sharpened, the entrenching tool was ideal for separating a German's head from the rest of the German in the trenches of WW I. But it had other uses as well. The store clerk, another ex-British soldier, said that an entrenching tool was a necessary complement to the function of the thunderbox. I took his word for this.

These purchases inspired me to go into Boots the Chemist and buy many bottles of kaolin and morphine mixture, then available in unlimited amounts without prescription. Before Imodium, kaolin and morphine mixture was the best known treatment for Montezuma's revenge. The chalky taste made it disgusting to swallow, but it was usually quickly effective, which made up for the taste. I also bought many rolls of loo paper.

———

Alyson and I were still seeing a lot of each other. She was busy with a new theatrical production, so I would meet her at a pub called The Salisbury that was next to the Albery Theatre. But the intensity of our affair had waned. Or so I thought.

A few days before we were about to leave, Alyson said to me, "I am afraid for you."

"Why?" I asked, thinking that she was worried about the drive.

"I think you are going to have a sad and lonely old age," Alyson said but didn't elaborate. I promised to write to her.

———

The day before we were to leave, Shelby announced to us that Julian, the ex-officer, wasn't going with us. It seemed that his mother had advised him not to. Shelby then said she assumed that the trip was off unless we could persuade Julian to change his mind.

Not so! The Honourable Jane shouted that the trip was on and that she wouldn't go with any adult male who let his mother make his decisions in any case. The ex-officer could go to hell. Lady Hester Stanhope and the others in *The Wilder Shores of Love* would have been proud of Jane. The blood of earls had spoken.

We left London as planned on June 17, 1971.

Off to a Bumbling Start

The first day on the German autobahn was ghastly. Rain poured down. Not only was Elsie's top speed in practice about 55 mph; her brick-like shape and peculiar weight distribution required constant fiddly steering adjustments as huge German trucks blasted past us, leaving the tail-heavy and poorly loaded Elsie swerving into the other lanes.

In pouring rain the first night, I offloaded all the cardboard boxes on the rear seat to find the tent, the sleeping bags, something to eat, and something to cook on. The next morning we struggled to reload everything so that Elsie's load would be roughly balanced between front and back. But we never quite achieved this, due to Dr. Porsche thoughtfully putting the engine in the rear.

Rain continued as we slogged down through Austria and into Yugoslavia. At first we all took turns driving, but Shelby's absentmindedness behind the wheel terrified Jane and myself, so Jane and I did most of the driving. A sullen silence gripped us. We passed wreck after wreck beside the Yugoslav Autoput, a raised two-lane road helpfully built by the Nazis to speed the transfer of German troops down into the Balkans. Yugoslavs used the Autoput to test their courage as drivers. The Yugoslav driving technique was one long game of chicken.

Bulgaria was a pleasant change. The sun came out and we opened the fabric sunroof. We drove through immense red fields of tomatoes and roses. The radio played non-stop throbbing "boy meets girl, girl meets tractor" Communist choral music that ends with the girl becoming "the little flower of the Five-Year Plan."

Eastward Ho!

At the Turkish border, the Turkish officials were cheerful, slow, and resolutely thorough. At least, unlike the Bulgarians, the Turks didn't insist on running the VW up onto a ramp to search the underside. But the Turks wanted all hippy travelers to know that Turkey had rules. Strict rules. Posters with the large, hard, wise face of Ataturk were next to signs that informed us, in a number of languages, that Turkey invariably executed drug dealers and always imprisoned drug users.

Otherwise, it was great to be in Turkey and wonderful to hear the cry from the mosques that "There is no God but God and Mohammad is His Prophet." We were in the East!

Jane and Shelby brightened up. Jane, I noticed, ate little, subsisting on many cups of sweetened coffee. Shelby waxed talkative. This was not an improvement. One of her chief topics of conversation was a detailed explanation of the troubles in Northern Ireland. I had never paid the slightest attention to them. The IRA had not yet done anything too awful in England. Had anyone asked me about Ireland prior to the trip, I would have mindlessly stated that justice was on the side of the Northern Irish Protestants.

Five hundred miles in the VW with Shelby soon made me question my ill-informed sympathy for the Irish Protestants, of whom Shelby was a born-and-bred adherent.

Shelby informed me that every true Irish Protestant could instantly tell who was an Irish Catholic by his or her eyes. She referred to Catholics as "taigs" in a completely matter-of-fact way. (Which was considered as offensive as the 'n' word.) The Catholics were becoming uppity and would need to be put back in their place. A group called the Orangemen, about whom I would hear much, would do the necessary putting back in place by whatever means were required.

Conveniently, as soon as we found a place to stay at the YMCA in Istanbul, we spent less time in each other's company. The first day, I went to Santa Sophia and lost myself in the great domed, white, silent interior. For me, Santa Sophia is the ultimate Christian structure, infinitely more moving than St. Peter's, that hulking rococo youngster in Rome. The dome of Santa Sophia looms above you in its infinite gloom, so vast and so knowing. All human folly has passed beneath.

Together, we went to the bazaar, then on to the Pudding Shop to post a notice that we were looking for a passenger. Everyone would see it. This otherwise nondescript modern restaurant was the meeting place for all Westerners who were launching themselves onto the hippie trail to the East.

The Pudding Shop features in many overland travel tales of the 1970s. Its role as the beginning of the hippie trail is described in Rory Maclean's fascinating recent book, *The Magic Bus*. This is an insightful, fun examination of the actions and motives of travelers like us who headed East way back then. Anyone wanting to know all about the hippie trail and its unkempt voyagers should read *The Magic Bus*.

Located right across from the magnificent Blue Mosque, in 1971 the Pudding Shop was full of every sort of traveler, ranging from gentle, utterly stoned and gloriously bearded freaks, to loud groups of American East Coast college girls, to crazy-eyed German anarchists of uncertain gender and on and on to chippy, working-class English guys with Rolling Stones hair-do's and guitars that they couldn't actually play.

The name of the Pudding Shop came from the rice pudding and other sweet things that were sold to assuage the munchies everyone had from smoking grass. We put up our notice and hung around for a while in an aimless way.

I wandered over to the Blue Mosque, built some thousand years after Santa Sophia. Even for me, an unbeliever, the mosque was just as moving and almost as vast as Santa Sophia. I chatted with the guard at the gate in a kind of Pidgin English. He gave me a pastry. Nice people, the Turks, thought I; every man looks like a soldier and acts like a new pal.

After dinner and several bottles of Buzbag, a cheap, glugable Turkish red wine that reminded me of Gallo Hearty Burgundy, Jane and Shelby got into a ding-dong argument about whether women should travel alone and, if so, what could they do safely. The Honourable Jane proved surprisingly cautious, at least for the purposes of this argument, advocating extreme care, especially at night.

Shelby said that there was no way that she would be shut in at night or at any other time. Shelby explained that she had been a shy, thin, awkward child; repressed and silent at school and naughty at home in compensation.

Life had begun for Shelby when she travelled alone in Mexico as a young, tall, blond student. A Mexican man whom she had just met burst into tears after some mild French kissing and promptly proposed to her. From Jane's look of amused disbelief, I took this to be an exaggeration, though Shelby was attractive in a blond, antiseptic way, and tall by Mexican standards.

Days in Istanbul were eventful. When I went into a barber's for a haircut, I was surprised that the barber, who looked like a US Marine gunnery sergeant, removed my shirt before proceeding. After a so-so haircut, I discovered why. He proceeded to wash— thoroughly and with lots of soap on a rather dirty towel—my ears, nose, eyes, and the inside of my mouth, followed by my neck and chest.

I went on to a mosque to watch the twelve o'clock prayers, then on to the Topkapi Palace, whose seraglio, or harem, was the final destination of Aimee Dubucq de Rivery, one of the remarkable women in *The Wilder Shores of Love*. Captured by the Barbary pirates, then sold into slavery, this blue-eyed, aristocratic French convent girl, Aimee, became the mistress of one sultan and the mother of one of the greatest, Mahmoud the Reformer. This great man saw to it that his mother had her death bed confession heard by a proper Catholic priest before she was buried as a Christian in an imperial turbeh (a grand raised tomb) not far from Santa Sophia. Prior to her burial, Aimee had not left the Seraglio for thirty-three years.

We took an old, slow steamboat up the Bosporus to look at the old mansions and wooden houses. Having already discovered that Turks did not like having their photos taken, Jane dodged around furtively, snapping the decrepit but striking ancient brown houses and ancient Turks of both sexes in and about the houses. The men were bareheaded and had big, weathered hands. The women were in black, always with a shawl over their heads.

At this point, a brisk, fit-looking woman of about forty stepped out from nowhere and loudly bawled out Jane for only photographing old things. The woman, who was completely Western in dress and fluent in English, told us, after calming down, that she was a medical doctor with a fine European medical training who wanted Turkey to be thought of as European and progressive. "After all," the woman said, "there are lots of new houses to photograph." The woman said nothing about not photographing old, shabby, traditionally dressed people.

Later I parked myself in a café. Shelby and Jane went off and returned with Jo and Orion. Jo was a soldier, a military policeman, and looked the part. A natural extrovert, Jo somewhat put me off by promptly informing me in guttural but understandable English that he could kill me with one blow of either hand.

Orion was a gloomy, pockmarked guy of twenty-seven who worked in the bazaar as a tourist tout and resented this. Previously, he spent three years as a waiter in Australia and the South Pacific and viewed this time as a lost paradise.

Jo and Orion took us to a good kebab house and then on to a whore house that doubled as a low-grade night club. I would have liked to see some good belly dancing, but Jo and Orion preferred something they considered sexy and European. We had smuggled in a large bottle of the cheapest Turkish brandy and drank it all furtively, while a dreadful local band attempted to play Western pop music. No one felt like dancing.

At some point, Jo and Orion must have decided that, even if Jo killed me with one blow, Jane and Shelby were unpromising sex targets, so they drifted off before the bill arrived. The three of us walked back to the depressing YMCA, stopping to look at the moonlight on the Bosporus. Somewhat drunk, Jane said that she needed to run away. I took her shoes and away she ran. At this point, Shelby took my arm. I wrote in my journal, "Hope it means nothing." And I added, "More thoughts about sex, love, and Alyson. Damn…"

"I am Lasse," said a deep male voice. I woke with a jolt in my cell at the YMCA to find a pencil-thin, tall, lugubrious Swede standing over me. Dressed in a dirty T-shirt and even dirtier jeans, with long, matted, dirty blond hair, this druggy character was the sole responder to our notice at the Pudding Shop. He was more than a little smelly.

We gathered over breakfast with our new passenger. Lasse, pronounced like the name of the canine TV star, wanted to travel with us for months; Lasse loved us all at first sight. Alas, he had only $140. So much for paying his way. Also, Lasse was plainly in the grip of some powerful chemical substance. But we said he could join us anyway. Since Lasse never spoke and we always drove with the windows open, we barely noticed him. He slipped away at a truck stop a few days later without saying bye-bye.

Leaving Istanbul, my journal becomes readable again. The YMCA cell didn't encourage me to write legibly; something about no table and the single overhead 40-watt light bulb, I suppose.

From my journal of June 28, 1971, near Gallipoli and June 29, 1971, near Eskishehir and June 30, 1971, at Sansum on the Black Sea:

Three days of hard driving, early departures, and difficult camping. We left Istanbul in the afternoon and drove most of the way to Gallipoli, camping on a plain below some low hills. After a tiny rain, we ate in the midst of a storm of insects.

Suddenly, up popped a young shepherd. Three hundred and thirty sheep were on the way, he signed. Did we mind? I decided that we didn't, gave him some whiskey and a cigar, and we talked as best we could. He has a simple, hard life, sleeping on the ground in his jacket and watching his flocks by night.

I drank too much and was stunned when Jane woke me at 5:30 a.m.

We visited the Gallipoli Monument near Cape Helles, the site of the initial landings in 1915. Looking at the narrow shingle beach beneath a steep hillside, I wondered if Churchill had done any geographic research or simply relied on his romantic views of military strategy. Struggling off the landing ship, the River Clyde, onto the rough gravel of the beach and up the hill with a seventy-pound pack under heavy fire would test the most resolute infantrymen. The casualties recorded on the monument, including many Indian soldiers, showed that the men did not falter. Of the first two hundred men who left the River Clyde, only twenty-one made it onto land alive.

We left Gallipoli in silence.

We drove hard all day in an effort to reach Ankara. The country was lovely, better watered than Greece and rather tidy. The roads, however, defeated us, and we were forced to stop at a BP gas station. It offered some simple camping facilities, as well as the hospitality of Mr. Orhan, the owner, his son, his brother, and assorted other relatives. Mr. Orhan kept insisting something about food. I assumed he wanted us to use his little restaurant. Shelby started cooking, until Mr. Orhan returned with tinned food, wine, and local cognac. I thought that he wanted us to buy this stuff, which I was willing to do.

But no, it was a gift. Mr. Orhan wanted us to get drunk and wallow in his hospitality. "Me capitalist," he said. Sick tired, I was longing for him to leave. Mr. Orhan seemed a little mad, producing drinks ranging from raki to a local horribly sweet banana liqueur, as well as various cigarette holders and souvenir key rings. Finally, he appeared in a full traditional Turkish rig, asking to be photographed. "Too dark," we said. "Wait until morning."

"Fine," he said indicating with his fingers that eight would do nicely.

It was a night of hell. There were large spiders everywhere and noise from the road and from a goddamned generator. At 6:00 a.m. we rose, and by 7:00 a.m. we were off, pulling out just as Mr. Orhan arrived, again in full kit. We took a few shots out of Elsie's windows. A generous loony.

Mr. Orhan had dressed himself again as a full-fledged whirling dervish, complete with a tall brown cap, a white robe with a cord around the waist, a dagger, and shoes with turned-up toes. I felt bad driving away, leaving this odd but good-natured man standing in front of his BP station, but leave we did.

The countryside was gorgeous: pale shades of green, rich browns, and reds against dramatic grey hills. We climbed up onto the Anatolian plateau that had wide plains like the American West, endless views, dry river beds, and a few shallow, fast-flowing rivers.

We camped for a night in Samsun on the Black Sea. The Turkish state-run campsite was pleasant enough, but a band played loud Turkish music until the wee hours.

I stayed up late reading Lord Kinross's terrific biography of Ataturk. Ataturk is little-known now outside of Turkey but was in every way the George Washington of modern Turkey. Winston

Churchill thought that Ataturk was one of the greatest men he ever met.

Ataturk was a superb soldier and came to power because of his success in holding off the Allied invasion of Gallipoli in 1915, then pushing out the invading Greek armies in the early 1920s after the Turkish defeat in World War I. Ataturk went on to create a secular Turkish state that was the first Islamic country to give rights to women.

Whatever his theoretical belief in female equality, Ataturk was a womanizer of heroic stature. Asked what he looked for in a woman, Ataturk replied, "Availability." When an Istanbul newspaper accused Ataturk of being a drunkard, he had a correction printed that stated "the President of Turkey is a drunkard and a lecher."

Having just visited Gallipoli, I could imagine what it was like in 1915 for Ataturk and his tough peasant soldiers dug in up on the heights, as the British and Australians, backed by massive naval gunfire, landed and tried to fight their way up the steep, scrub-filled ravines. Their goal was to push the Turks off the tops and free the British navy to sail up the straits into Istanbul. That was the moment when Ataturk wrote in his diary: "The weight of responsibility is heavier than death." Ataturk and his men held the heights.

On the Black Sea coast, we stopped to watch some boys stage a swimming festival. The beach had dark sand. As usual, no girls were in evidence.

Along the Black Sea coast, the country is hilly, and on July 1 it had an almost-tropical feel. We wound along a slow road that tracked the indentations of the coast. The little towns were mean. We camped with difficulty on a rocky ledge above a beach. In my journal I wrote that "the camp was nice enough at night, but come dawn I instantly became the lord of the flies, so we left at 5:30 a.m."

Driving along the coast, we found an apparently deserted beach at Treboli where the sea was clear with a rocky bottom. We went in for a dive with masks and snorkels and came up to find ourselves among about twenty boys aged nine or ten who were a lot of fun. We got out and talked with the kids in our now familiar mixture of

Turkish and English. In those days, Turks were extremely friendly and curious about strangers and not inhibited by language problems. The boys wanted to talk about European soccer and America. Treboli was a delightful place of old, tumbled-down houses, a castle, and a funny cloud that appeared like a Scotch mist at exactly 11:00 a.m. and promptly disappeared again.

By now the heat and humidity were ferocious. We pushed on to Trabzon. Despite my love for Rose Macaulay's elegant comic novel *The Towers of Trebizond*, the actual Trabzon held no magic, and we were relieved to drive inland, back onto the high plateau of Anatolia. The country looked like the Pyrenees. We stopped for drinking water, but I forgot to gas up. We climbed and climbed, oohing and aahing over the views, until we reached the top of a six-thousand-foot pass. There I noticed that we were more or less out of gas.

A man at the pass said that it was twenty-five kilometers to the next gas station. We coasted down the other side, trying not to fry Elsie's feeble drum brakes. Finally finding a solitary gas pump with a kid attending it, we started to look for a camp site. I was beginning to wonder whether camping just any old place in the middle of rural Turkey with two girls was a wise idea. Formal camp sites in interior Turkey in 1971 were few and far between, as was even the most modest sort of hotel. The locals seemed friendly enough, but some of the hippies we met were totally nuts—and not in an amusing way. Who knew who might be passing through at night?

So I was relieved when, just before dark, I spotted an apple orchard between the road and the river we were tracking downhill. I found the Turk who ran the orchard. Sporting a splendid traditional mustache and the look of a Turkish warrior chief, this fine man was one of nature's gentlemen, kind and generous and full of fun. We spent the evening drinking local wine and raki, listening to the man and his friend sing old Turkish songs with tuneful feeling. I wrote after the performance, "I love this country."

On July 3, near Erzurum on the road to Iran, we had a nerve-wracking encounter. The country was poor and rocky. We noticed that the people were much less friendly. Some boys threw rocks at Elsie as we drove by, but they missed. Women we passed pulled their dark head shawls across their faces.

Therefore, we stopped well outside any town to have our usual lunch of local bread and dehydrated soup for Shelby and me, and coffee only for Jane. (Despite eating nothing most of the time, Jane insisted quietly but firmly on doing most of the cooking.)

We were sitting on the road verge next to Elsie when a tractor drove up, with a young, tough-looking man riding on the rear fender next to the driver. The man was stocky, about thirty-two or thirty-three, wearing a short-sleeved shirt and khaki slacks. He was neat and had a crew cut. No mustache. No hat. A modern Turk.

The guy hopped off the fender and waved the tractor on. He sat down with us without being asked but smiled politely and asked in good English how we were. Jane instantly warmed to this guy. I had exactly the opposite reaction. Especially after he showed us his identity card as a plain clothes police captain and the snub-nosed .38 Smith and Wesson revolver that he wore in an ankle holster. This was definitely someone I did not want to get to know better. We chatted for a while. The cop acted friendly and open. So, naturally, the Honourable Jane immediately accepted his invitation to go back to his police station for an after-lunch drink.

We drove, with him in the passenger seat, back down the road a mile or so and turned off into a one-story compound with a courtyard. A sign in front stated that it was indeed a police barracks. We went into an office where the cop drew up chairs and offered us glasses of milky yoghurt and water. Nervously I sipped the drink, though I hate yoghurt in any form. The policeman passed around a box of cheap, strong Turkish cigarettes. I lit up one of these, though I don't smoke cigarettes. Anything to keep this guy smiling.

At that point the cop suggested that we might like to make a tour of his prison cells. Shelby and I looked at each other in horror as Jane said brightly that there was nothing she would like more. As soon as

Jane and the policeman left the room, I grabbed Shelby by the arm, and we rushed back to Elsie. We started Elsie up, agreed that we would go back in if Jane didn't appear in ten minutes, and sat in silent fear. My assumption was that if something happened to Jane, we also would be inconvenient to have around any longer. So we might as well go in after her.

Five very long minutes later, Jane came rushing out with her hand over her mouth. Shelby hopped out and hustled Jane into the VW Bus, at which point Jane burst into floods of tears. I took off before Jane could explain what happened. We drove for what seemed like hours in silence, apart from Jane's sobs.

After a while, when no one came after us, Jane explained what had happened. The policeman had led Jane into a cell, immediately pushed her up against the wall and, without a word, put his hand down the front of her jeans and forcefully groped her. Jane spun away and rushed out of the building to us. She was crying from humiliation and from anger that she had misjudged the situation, not from fear. Jane was brave.

Possibly we overreacted in imagining that this rural policeman would come after us. The policeman had probably never been out of Turkey and had heard that Western hippie girls were an easy make. But something could have gone horribly wrong all too easily. No one knew where we were; there were no cell phones in those days. We would not have gotten far in Elsie if they had come after us in anything faster—which was almost anything else with wheels and a motor.

For the next few days, we could see Mount Ararat; first from a great distance, then in its full dramatic, snow-crowned glory. A perfect volcanic cone, Mount Ararat rises from a high, treeless plain to 5137 meters, or 16,854 feet. The weather was perfect, and the effect was like IMAX. Few people were in the area, though we occasionally passed small groups of tribal folk. The tribal women were dressed brightly in reds and yellows and made no attempt to cover their faces, possibly because they were too busy with their children, sheep, and goats.

Exploring Iran

We entered Iran after a long delay but without problems and drove to Tabriz. After Turkey, Iran was flat and monotonous. The land was brown, stony, arid, and more-or-less useless. Tabriz is largely Turkish and had a modern feel to it. We pushed on quickly from Tabriz to find the real Iran.

Iranian food seemed a little monotonous too, after the rich variety of Turkish food. As in Turkey, we ate in truck stops where we could go into the kitchen and see what was simmering or order something from a glass-fronted refrigerated cabinet. But there didn't appear to be all the variations on eggplant that I had loved in Turkey. Given our method of travel, plus Jane's reluctance to eat anything solid, it is more than likely that we missed out on the more subtle aspects of Iranian food.

I found myself eating chello kebabs over and over again. These consist of coarsely minced, spicy lamb cooked as a kebab and served on top of a large plate of buttered white rice. Delicious.

Iranian bread is also marvelous. It is baked in an outdoor beehive-shaped oven fired by wood. The baker slaps the round piece of unleavened dough against the sloping inside of the oven with a wooden paddle, then retrieves it when it is a lovely golden color on each side. It is perfect on its own or with honey.

Tehran made a poor initial impression on us, which was confirmed by later events. Though there were occasional views of attractive mountains to the north of Tehran, the city itself had the sprawling charm of Tulsa, Oklahoma.

We spent July 6 to July 8 in a dump of a campsite in the outskirts of the city. A nearby VW shop serviced Elsie cheaply and quickly. We went into Tehran to look at the Shah's crown jewels, found them closed, then on to American Express where I was crushed not to find a letter from Alyson.

Possibly this was why my tension with Shelby began to shift into a more active phase. Shelby nagged Jane constantly about Jane's eating problem. Idiot that I was, I had never heard of anorexia and merely thought that Jane was picky. Jane looked thin but healthy. I felt that the nagging achieved nothing. Let Jane be Jane.

The dynamics of travelling with two highly competent women posed problems that I was grossly ill-suited to deal with. I considered myself a feminist, at least by the low male standard of 1971. Jane and Shelby could do most things that I could do, but I understood that Jane and Shelby also appreciated occasional doses of patronizing male behavior to keep their own feminist faith alive. They also wanted me to load and unload Elsie and to make camp. It was all very confusing.

The feminism of the 1960s was long overdue but left these bright women—and me—unsure what the new rules of the game were. A woman could now do her own thing, but what was her own thing? Was neurotic "oh little me" behavior still permissible? Were logic and emotional control by definition macho? If so, was it alright to act irrationally? Or to let it all go emotionally? One set of rules was junked, but where did you find the new rules?

Despite the myriad character defects of any male, Shelby wanted a man. This led to her obsession with combing through the male hippies at our every stop, claiming that it was essential to find paying passengers. But after a day or two of some character riding with us, Shelby would find some reason to fire the guy. Jane, who could have had her pick of hippie men, showed no interest in them.

We drove south to Isfahan. Iranian desert roads were dead straight and well surfaced; gasoline was dirt cheap, so we drove flat out at our top speed of fifty miles per hour.

Despite the straight roads, driving in Iran was stressful. There was always the chance of being turned into a fireball by some long-distance trucker in an immense, brand new Mercedes truck that would appear first as a little dot way down the road with heat shimmers around it. The truck would appear to be driven by a normal, rational driver and to be in the appropriate lane.

As he neared us, the driver would suddenly swerve out of his lane and come thundering down the middle of the road, requiring instant evasive action by whoever was driving Elsie. The trucks always just missed us, but we saw many burnt-out wrecks along the roadside. And we also saw multi-vehicle wrecks that were clearly the result of a head-on collision followed by a secondary crash from behind; it was hard to comprehend how this happened on such straight, sparsely travelled roads.

My impression was that the average Iranian truck driver in 1971 had gone directly from piloting a donkey in his village to being behind the wheel of a massive German or Swedish truck. Add a large dose of inshallah, and bad stuff happens.

Iran is almost the size of Alaska, the largest state in the United States. The long periods of boredom while driving slowly in great heat through scrubby wastelands made the three of us wax philosophical. Apart from watching the approach of an occasional dust devil, there was nothing near the road to see. And on the occasions when a sandstorm converged with us, there was nothing at all to see for several minutes. So we talked. Since none of us had much interest in abstract morality or theories of cognition, we talked about the purpose of travel and about why a traveler should keep a journal.

Jane felt strongly that the point of travel was self-discovery. To achieve this, the traveler should meet as many people of all different types as possible. By talking with these people, and by sympathetically trying to understand them and why they were different from you and from the culture of your home, you learned about yourself. Shelby thought that learning firsthand about culturally diverse people was in itself sufficient to change the way you viewed life and the world.

I basically agreed with Jane and Shelby. We weren't tourists; we saw no point in travel as travelogue: taking lots of photos while noting the little mosque over there, the cart of the quaint fruit seller with the big nose opposite the mosque, or the rich blue of the remaining cracked tiles on the minaret.

However, understanding Iranians in a sympathetic way was not easy. The problem was not wholly language. Many Iranians in the cities spoke English. Our contacts with Iranians were more and more perplexing and unsatisfactory as we drove further into the country. Unlike Tabriz, where most of the population were of Turkish origin, or Tehran, which was cosmopolitan, we were now in the real Persian heartland.

Whatever their actual job, the men we encountered all apparently aspired to be crooked rug dealers. Ordinary Iranians were superficially friendly but needed constant watching. At gas stations, if you gave the pump attendant the equivalent of a five-dollar bill, you had to count every small coin he handed back or else you were short-changed every single time. The amounts they pocketed were trivial; this was a game. The Iranians deluded themselves; they thought they were acting like Armenians or Jews, whom they envied but claimed to despise. However, Armenians and Jews don't cheat. They haggle fiercely, but once they have made a deal they deliver.

There was a melancholy about Iranians. When unaware that we were watching them, the men looked gloomy, even when strolling hand in hand with other young men. (Even Iranian army officers strolled hand in hand.)

Of course, for ordinary Iranians, there was little in Iranian history to be cheerful about and little mirth in the Shia version of Islam, which most Iranians practice, either. Shia suffering started with the martyrdom of Ali, whom the Shiites believe was the rightful heir to Muhammad, in 661 AD. The Sunni majority in other Islamic countries made sure that their Shia neighbors had plenty of reasons to remember Ali's agony over the next thirteen centuries. And if Shias need further reminders of how their martyrs suffered, there are annual opportunities for flagellation. Like Calvinism, Shia Islam is not a sect for the lighthearted.

Isfahan was a gorgeous artistic delight. I'd been to Cairo and Granada. Both are full of the most wonderful examples of Islamic architecture, but Isfahan surpasses them. Isfahan is only the third-largest city of Iran but was the Persian capital under the Safavid rulers. It peaked in the sixteenth century under Shah Abbas the Great (1587–1629) when it was one of the largest cities in the world. Located on the Zayandeh-Rud River, there are bridges with dozens of pointed arches dating from that time. The success of Isfahan was due to its position on the east–west trade routes of the time.

The central Naghsh-e Jahan Square is one of the largest and most beautiful civic squares in the world. Jane and I wandered around it for hours.

The bazaar abuts the square, and there Jane demonstrated her considerable skill in haggling. With her help and by walking away several times, I bought for a reasonable price some blue traditional pottery with black markings that Alyson and I still have. The heat was intense but bearable under the colonnade around the great Square. We went to the Chehel Sotoun, the Palace of the Forty Columns. Twenty of the columns are reflections of the twenty actual wooden columns in the pool in front of the Palace.

As a distraction, that night we went to a spaghetti Western, mostly to get out of the heat for a while. The dialog was dubbed into Farsi, but the film was easy to follow.

I noted in my journal that, in an effort to get Shelby to stop sharing the driving, I told her one morning—honestly—that "I had a dream about her tipping the bus over, then refusing to get out so that we all burned." I didn't record her response.

We then drove south to Shiraz, famous for its poets and its roses. On the way we planned to go to Persepolis, one of the greatest classical sites. Unfortunately, the Shah decided to have an enormous celebration to hail the 2500th anniversary of the founding of the Persian Empire, thus highlighting his role as the current glorious incumbent of the Peacock Throne.

Though the celebration wasn't until October, Persepolis was closed for preparations and vermin removal. The Iranian Army was exterminating every snake, spider, and scorpion on the site so that foreign dignitaries would not have any unpleasant experiences, like having a snake climb their leg as they took their first mouthful of caviar.

The spending on this gala was so over the top that it is often cited as the beginning of the end for the Shah's reign. My impression was that the Shah was already intensely hated by the lower two-thirds of society, carrying on another ancient Persian tradition.

Shiraz was a total write-off for me. As soon as we arrived, I felt bad enough to be in Cleveland. I immediately had the most violent attack of vomiting and gut rot of my whole life (and I have had many). I spent two days and nights lying on a cot in the dormitory of a youth hostel along with other afflicted male Western travelers, shouting in agony for them to clear the way when I needed the only loo. (The loo, of course, was a hole in the floor—the horrid "Persian version.") I did a lot of this shouting and drank many bottles of kaolin and morphine.

Upon recovering, I went to find a possible fellow traveler, a German who had caught Shelby's eye. My search was a waste of time since, out of diffidence or shyness, she failed to get his name or where he was staying. But he sounded promising. By this time we realized that, since we were all on the hippie trail, we would see the same people again and again, so we didn't worry too much about missing him.

We drove slowly back to Tehran. By this time, the tummy curse was affecting all of us. At each of our frequent stops, one of us would grab the thunderbox, slip one of our remaining rolls of loo paper over the shaft of the entrenching tool and head off into the scrubland. Anthony Kershaw's recommendation that we should not leave the UK without a thunderbox was simply invaluable. Using as a slogan: "The thunderbox; Don't Leave Home without It;" I could have sold dozens of them along the way.

In Tehran, I found a letter from Alyson waiting. Shelby found her German. So we both were ecstatic, though it was clear from Alyson's letter that none of my letters had reached her. The German had his own VW Bus, a German army surplus one still painted Bundeswehr olive green, with a small German flag on the rear bumper. We decided to go in informal convoy on to Afghanistan.

On July 17, we drove north from Tehran to the Caspian Sea. The drive was spectacular; it went along a raging stream up and up until a series of tunnels took us to a high dam. Despite the heat, the country was a brilliant green, unlike the rest of summertime Iran. We crossed the watershed and followed another stream that flowed down to the Caspian. That night we couldn't find a camp, so we squatted in an unfinished resort development.

The next morning was spent replacing a tire I had ruined by driving on it after it was flat. On the way to Gorgan, we stopped and went into an Iranian farming village that was just a little way off the main road. The buildings were neat, and many were new. The village had electricity and running water and a few TV antennas. There was a reasonably well-equipped school, at least in terms of books and desks and plenty of large pictures of the Shah inside and outside. Lots of children followed us cheerfully about. The few adults in sight were less pleased to see us, so we didn't stay long.

In Gorgan we found no place to camp, but we were finally directed to a peculiar site some miles outside of town. We forded a stream on the way there, and then by flashlight pitched camp in a newly paved parking lot. In 1971, there were many housing developments in attractive areas of Iran at various stages of completion. This development had begun, and apparently ended, with building the large parking lot where we camped.

The parking lot also contained a number of cars that were stationary with their engines idling. In the West, this would have been a lover's lane; here all the occupants were pairs of young men smoking grass. We immediately became an object of interest. They put their car headlights on us. I suppose they wanted to be sure that we were merely foreign travelers, not secret policemen.

Once we convinced the locals to stop putting their high beams on us, it was a pleasant enough place to spend the evening. We sat on the curb at the edge of the paving. Small, green frogs came out of little holes in the ground to watch us, just as some of the locals came over from their cars. We sat and talked for hours. The locals were students in their late teens. In broken English, they told us many ugly stories about the Shah's Iran.

A friend of one of the students was "disappeared" as in Stalin's Russia. After this happened to someone, his name vanished from the school register and from everywhere else. If his mother went to the police to ask about this unfortunate person, she was told that no one had ever heard of him. And it was wiser not to go and ask.

In the cool of the morning, we set off eastwards, heading for Mashhad, the second city of Iran. Initially the scenery was green and the drive pleasing, but we soon ran out of paved road and ate hot dust for hours, bouncing along at about twenty miles per hour. We couldn't face stopping for lunch and drove on. Finally, we decided to stop at a miserable town named Shirvan but found that the only conceivable place to stay, a hotel, was run by extortionists. So we drove on and on, finally camping in the grounds of a government-run inn at Quchan. The night was clear and the semi-desert freezing cold after dark.

Jane went to bed without eating anything. Shelby told me again of her great concern about Jane. Cretin that I was, I repeated my belief that Jane would spontaneously snap out of it in her own good time. That evening, I realized that one of Shelby's motives in coming on the trip was to keep an eye on Jane. Perhaps there were good qualities in Shelby under the Ulster Protestant carapace? She was trying to be a good friend to Jane.

Mashhad is the second-largest city in Iran. The shrine of Imam Reza, in the center of Mashhad, is immense and of the greatest religious significance for Shiites, making Mashhad probably the second- or third-most-visited holy site in the Muslim world. Millions of pilgrims visit the city every year.

The theological differences between the two main branches of Islam—Sunni and Shiite—are subtle and many and quite beyond my ability to discuss in any detail. (Of course, simply being aware that such a division exists would have been of enormous help to our great military strategists in Washington DC.) At the most basic level, these differences involve an utter disagreement about who were the legitimate spiritual heirs to the Prophet Muhammad. Shias believe that there were twelve blood successors to Muhammad who were his rightful heirs. This Shia tradition is sometimes called "Twelver." Sunnis believe in another line of succession.

Few of the twelve Imams died peacefully, since orthodox Islamic religious and political forces wanted them dead. Imam Reza was the eighth Imam and, per custom, was poisoned in 818 AD. His tomb is housed in a most magnificent shrine with an enormous gilded dome over the tomb. The whole shrine complex is surrounded by a circular wall with stretches of elaborate iron fence through which non-believers can view the shrine. The main bazaar is right outside the shrine.

Mashhad was a likable city of long, tree-shaded avenues and little cool corners and squares. We immediately met some friendly students who wanted to show us how rugs are made. We were firm, though, and said that we must see the great shrine before we did anything else. The students warned us to be respectful and careful around the shrine. The students, all male, were somewhat dubious about the wisdom of Jane and Shelby going near the shrine.

Grudgingly, Jane and Shelby turned two large towels into do-it-yourself chadors. The chador is the Persian shawl that women drape over their heads then hold with one hand across their bodies. Nowadays, we are used to photos of Iranian women wearing black chadors. In those days, black chadors were uncommon. The shah had banned chadors altogether but with limited success. In 1971 in Tehran, younger women all wore Western clothes. Mashhad was more traditional, but we thought that a gesture would suffice. Two reluctant towel-headed females and I set off for the shrine.

Apart from the towels, Jane and Shelby were, as usual, braless in T-shirts and jeans. Passing through the bazaar on the way into the shrine, we attracted some unwelcome attention. I dropped a few steps behind the two women to keep an eye on things as we entered the shrine. The atmosphere was not pleasant. There is an undercurrent among devout Shias that isn't exactly threatening but suggests that collective hysteria isn't far from the surface.

The shrine was fabulous; the amount of gold leaf all over the dome blasted back the bright July sun and heat. I was absent-mindedly half-looking at the dome as we were carried along with the crowd. When I turned to pay attention to where we were going, I noticed that a kid who appeared to be about ten or eleven (which meant that he was actually about fourteen) had slipped between me and Shelby. And without so much as a "please, foreign lady, may I grope you," this little bastard reached forward and the goose went in, right up between Shelby's legs.

Without a thought, I stepped forward and gave the little scumbag an open-handed swat—hard—across the back of his head. The kid must have thought that Allah had intervened, having not noticed me. He stumbled, nearly fell, and gave a shout of fear.

Instantly, I realized that I had done something truly stupid. There was muttering among the men around us in the crowd. Fortunately, one guy had witnessed the whole thing and thought it was extremely funny. He started laughing, and others did too. The men jeered at the kid, at which point we made a swift exit from the shrine.

Jane then bawled me out for another act of cultural insensitivity. Suicidal idiocy was more like it.

While we were wandering around, the "students" found us again. Whether all or any of the young men we met in Iran were the students they claimed to be, I will never know. Certainly many of them were also touts for bazaar merchants. These were no exception. They took me to several shops run by sinister, fat Sidney Greenstreet-types before presenting me to two pleasant-looking young guys named Abbas and Hossein, who owned a small shop above a little courtyard.

The shop was piled high with rolled-up carpets. I was given a delicious Turkish coffee and made to feel like the buyer for Harrods or Bloomingdales as carpet after carpet was unrolled for me to inspect. Abbas and Hossein were only in their late twenties. The shop was fascinating. There were several men seated cross-legged, skillfully repairing carpets.

Everything was explained to me. Abbas and Hossein mostly bought carpets in villages where the patterns were Baluchi and Turkoman. Individual weavers were jealous about protecting their patterns and their skills and were often rude and difficult to bargain with. On top of this, Abbas and Hossein had a new and original gripe about the Shah. They believed that the Shah's education program would keep boys from going into rug making. Boys who could read weren't keen on spending their days knotting rugs.

After some lengthy haggling, I bought a "genuine" cherry silk Turkoman for $105. When I later took it to be cleaned in London by Bernadout, a famous London rug dealer, Mr. Bernadout himself informed me that the carpet was made of the finest rayon and only worth cleaning for its souvenir value. And so I learned more about carpets than I had bargained for. Silly me; I had even written in my journal: "Most disappointing if my new pals turn out to be dishonest." But at the time, I was highly chuffed by my purchase, and to celebrate I went off to swim with the students. The pool was public and free. To get a swimsuit, you left a shoe. The pool was large and clean and full of screaming Iranians, but males only, aged from ten to twenty. It was odd to swim in a really big, crowded outdoor pool without a single female.

After the swim, the pack of touts drifted away. I was down to two students who actually just wanted to talk. Both were highly fed up with their lives. The older, a dark, quiet boy of about nineteen or twenty was contemptuous of the pilgrims to the shrine and a cynic about Islam. He said, "Man goes to Mecca a dog and returns a wolf." He didn't think much of the Shahanshah—Shah of Shahs—either. To leave the country, as he hoped to do someday soon, a man had to complete military service, pay $300 in tax, and post a $1400 bond in case the man didn't return to Iran. Few ever returned.

That evening we were reunited with Shelby's German doctor. Friede turned out to be a young guy of about my age; he was a slender, handsome man of medium height, brown hair, and blue eyes. In appearance he was pure North German.

His bus, though plain German army surplus on the outside, was fitted out inside with a sleeping place for Friede and a companion, plus a good deal of medical equipment, including a surprising number of green glass medical bottles containing Friede's own blood plasma. Friede thought that the greatest risk from a third-world auto accident, apart from any injuries, was the local medical care after the accident. He intended to treat himself if at all possible. I had a vision of Friede gnawing his leg off like a fox in a trap but kept it to myself.

Apart from the usual drugs a doctor would carry, Friede also had a wide selection of recreational drugs. Friede produced what we instantly called a "chockie bikkie;" it was a small, round, hard disk of gummy hashish that looked just like a British chocolate-covered biscuit. Friede broke off a chunk, crumbled this up, fiddled the tobacco out of a filter cigarette, mixed the hash with some tobacco, and tamped the mixture back into the filter cigarette. Then we lit up and passed the joint around.

Unlike President Bubba Clinton, I had both tried and inhaled grass many times before but always found the effect mild. This hashish was different. Jane thought the hash was mixed with opium. After a few drags, I was in another world. I found myself discussing the possibilities of a world of perfect peace and universal harmony with Friede. Then Friede and I went for a long, long moonlit walk to a far away tree, locked in mutual understanding and trust. We floated over what appeared to be massive rocks. It took hours to reach the tree and more hours to return to the camp.

Exhausted from the long walk, I felt a strong need to lie down. Dreams in magical colors whirled me around inside them; thoughts of the maddest sex with Alyson engulfed me—over and over again. It was a night of wonders. And it was more than pinks and violets and dreams of sex; I knew violently, fully, totally, to the core of my being that I could not live without Alyson.

In the morning I noticed that the tree was about twenty feet away from where Friede and I had started. The rocks were the size of a fist. But I couldn't stop thinking about Alyson.

I Encounter Iranian Justice

Before leaving Mashhad, we visited the tomb of Ferdowsi, one of the greatest Persian poets. The tomb was modern, with multilingual inscriptions that linked the Shah to the glories of ancient Persian culture. The buried poet was incidental.

That same day, July 24, we reached Taybad, the last town in Iran before the Afghan border. The heat was beyond ferocious. There was no cover and no place to camp, so we went to a small, modern cement-block building that passed for a hotel. Taybad was a dump. The buildings were new but already run down. Fine dust covered everything, churned up by the numerous Russian motorcycles that appeared at great speed from nowhere, ran flat out through Taybad, and disappeared again into the distance. There wasn't a tree or a hill or bush or anything green in sight.

Walking down the dismal and only street with small dust devils accompanying us, we agreed that we were anxious to reach Afghanistan. In a loud, upper-class English bray, Jane blamed anything and everything that was wrong with Iran on the Shah.

In response, I speculated whether the Iranians themselves might have played some role in creating the society that in turn produced the Shah. Would getting rid of the Shah make much difference, I asked? Would the mullahs with their thirteenth-century worldview be any better? The students were obviously totally out to lunch and certain to get shafted, whatever else happened. Perhaps the Iranians were their own worst enemies? Maybe Iran was just a dud society? Possibly Shia Islam warped people's thinking? The looks I received told me that these comments were a mistake.

After dinner that evening, Jane, Shelby, and Friede took turns in rubbishing me at length for believing that Western culture had the slightest value. Since we were all drunk and befuddled with hashish, the debate is a little hard to recreate, but bear with me. It was a discussion that I heard or participated in over and over, all along the hippie trail.

Friede, whom I was beginning to like and respect, took a "more in sorrow than in anger" approach to me that I found hard to counter. If I would simply let go, and just feel, all would be revealed. Throw away all the constipating conventions of the West. Embrace love and feeling.

But let go of what? A belief in the superiority of flush toilets? A belief in the stern God of my Presbyterian ancestors that I would first have to acquire in order to lose? Would growing a beard help? Friede said patiently that I didn't need to know what to let go of; I simply needed to feel more. Just feel the spirit of the universe. I had to work on it. Smoking hash would help, but I had to work harder at feeling.

There was something Hegelian, some Geist here that I needed to imbibe or to absorb. I halfheartedly but sincerely promised Friede to try to feel more. I was bad; I was the Mr. Gradgrind of our small spiritual community, sucking out the good karma with treacherous thoughts about Hume and Adam Smith. I vowed to try harder. And I sincerely meant it at the time.

The next morning, July 25, we rushed to the border crossing, wanting to see the backside of Taybad ASAP.

We went into a small, windowless border police building. The interior had neon lighting and, despite the gloom, was about the temperature of the sun's surface. A policeman was sitting behind a metal desk with a fan behind him. The policeman was wearing a uniform that was a cross between that of an American state trooper and the doorman at a fine old London hotel. He wore almost opaquely dark Ray-Bans. He motioned Friede forward, flipped through his passport and VW documents, stamped them, and waved him through. Then Jane and Shelby were stamped and waved through. I watched them go through the door on the border side.

I stepped forward politely and handed over my documents. The policeman looked at them carefully, especially my passport's Iranian visa. Then he spoke for the first time since we had all walked in.

"You stay," he said.

I was baffled. "Why?" I said.

"You overstay visa." I looked at the Iranian visa in my passport. He was right. When Jane had taken our passports to the Iranian consulate, she and Shelby had received ninety-day visas. Mine was only for three weeks. The dates were in Persian numerals so I hadn't realized this in London. Now I understood it only too well.

"But the two women are with me. They are my women," I said. This was a powerful argument in Iran, I thought.

"They go. You stay. They are okay," he said.

"But they are traveling in my VW Bus."

"No, VW will stay too."

"What do I do now?" I asked.

"You go to court when judge comes back."

"How long will that be?" I asked.

The policeman gave me an evil smile. He was enjoying this. Probably he hated infidels and hippies in equal parts.

"Maybe a week. Maybe a month."

"But where can I stay?"

"Hotel in Taybad. Not to leave Taybad."

The policeman then explained that I was to go back to Taybad. I could go on foot from one end of the main (and only) street to the other end, all of a thousand yards. I asked if I could take photos. "If you want camera smashed," was the answer. I could consider myself arrested.

Jane and Shelby had come back into the building. They sized up the situation fast. They would go on with Friede to Herat. If I didn't catch up with them within a few days, they would tell the American consul, assuming that there was one.

Feeling dismal, I went back to the grotty hotel. I could only afford to stay there for a few days. I walked up and down the street, looking at the cement-block buildings. Taybad had an eccentric collection of businesses: two dry cleaners, two kebab shops, two banks, and a photographer. Just outside the town was a large, old mud-brick fort that I didn't dare to walk to.

Up one side of the street I walked, down the other, until I felt tired. I then slept fitfully in the heat of the hotel room all afternoon.

What followed was, as my journal puts it, "one of the most unusual evenings of my life." I went down to the restaurant, washed down a kebab with a large dose of Iranian vodka—cheap and excellent—and was glumly rereading a novel of Trollope's. I was the only person in the restaurant, which was brightly lighted and featured the usual glass-fronted refrigerated cabinet full of kebabs, small fish and melons; there were also some Formica-topped tables and metal chairs.

At about nine in the evening, without warning, quite a number of people came in at the same time. They were a bizarre assortment. They were: a buttoned-down, young American married couple straight from some college in Indiana; an Iranian army major; a couple of what I took to be Savak, or Iranian secret policemen; a youngish Iranian civilian in a short-sleeved white shirt whom the others deferred to; two apparent bodyguards of the civilian; and a guy who played the role of court jester to the civilian. The court jester had the most remarkable forty-five degree slope to his forehead, a shaved head, and many tattoos.

The Savak were the Shah's Gestapo or KGB, numerous and widely feared. There were thousands of actual Savak and more thousands of willing and unwilling informers. The Shah's Iran was a police state of a peculiar sort, lenient in odd ways, cruel and unpredictable in others. Basically, being secular, apolitical and middle class were the correct things to be under the Shah. Making money was okay; being poor or thinking too much about Allah wasn't.

Despite the lack of any obvious connections among this gang, they pulled several tables together and sat down as a group. The court jester produced a battery phonograph from behind the bar and a pile of 45 rpm records. He started playing old pre-Beatles American hits like "Twenty-Four Hours from Tulsa" and "Baby Love." The effect on me was beyond depressing.

My feelings must have shown on my face, because after a few minutes the court jester came over to me. "Why don't you join nice party?" he asked. I said that ever since I was arrested, I hadn't been feeling very cheerful.

"You are arrested? Come and talk to judge," said the jester.

Yes, the young civilian in the white shirt was the travelling judge (and one who could briskly arrange a good, swift hanging.) But that evening he was a bubbly, friendly judge who wanted everyone to be happy. I went over to his table. The judge first established that my religion wasn't Judaism. He looked at my passport. He asked me about musical trends in the UK. Then he gave me a large shot of vodka, told me to be ready to go to the police station and to have fun in the meantime. Why didn't I dance? So I did.

I would have instantly stripped butt-assed naked if he'd asked.

Somewhat later, the court jester told me that he would drive me to the police station. He indicated that a small financial contribution would be appropriate.

We went outside and got into a military jeep. I slipped the jester twenty dollars and put another twenty dollars inside my passport. We drove some hundred and fifty feet down the street, back to the border police station. My policeman pal, wearing the same opaque Ray Bans and the same US state trooper's uniform, took my passport, slipped the money into his pocket, and stamped my passport. I hopped back into the jeep, and I was driven the hundred and fifty feet back to the hotel.

When I rejoined the party, the two Savak men had formed a duet and were singing English and American pop songs tunefully. I thanked the judge, who gave me several more large vodkas. Eventually we all went to bed royally drunk. I never found out why this strange party had turned up. I didn't trust myself to talk with the American couple.

The next day I discovered that the police had taken the rotor arm out of the distributor of the VW. Somehow, I didn't feel like going back to my Ray Ban–wearing pal to ask for it. I had a spare one, so I put it in the distributor and drove off immediately. I crossed the border with only a routine six-hour hold-up and was at last in Afghanistan.

Afghanistan—The First Time

Entering Afghanistan by land gives even the most blasé Westerner culture shock. There were no uniforms on the border guards, whose inspection of travelers was cursory. There was a dust-covered, once green-striped flag that was so tattered that it could have been the flag of any Islamic country. The land was brown; the official buildings were made of mud bricks. There was no sign of human habitation apart from these border shacks.

Then I noticed that a bearded man in a turban, with one eye missing and a facial hideousness like a slap, was standing near me, silently watching me. The man was dressed in layers of ragged clothes. In fact, quite a number of men in ragged clothes were standing about, all silently watching me. Their look was blank, neither curious nor uncurious.

These were men of a variety that I had never before seen, even as an enlisted man in the US Army. The draft dragged many odd-looking American men out of the nooks and crannies of our vast country. But these Afghan men were different beyond anything I'd experienced. Every traveler I talked to, both then and later, was struck by this rich Afghan goulash of human diversity.

Some Afghans appeared Asiatic, with slanted eyes and high cheekbones. Some appeared like characters out of Lawrence of Arabia with long, biblical beards and hawk's beak noses. Some had fair hair and light skin. Some had the most dramatic facial pockmarks I have ever seen, which I took to be the result of smallpox. Some were tall, but we also saw quite a few dwarves. Some men wore turbans. Others wore embroidered round caps. Some had fine white teeth. Some had a mouth full of blackened stumps. There was no pattern.

Observing Afghan men made it clear that Afghanistan is an ethnic mishmash. This is the core reason why Afghanistan is not a country but a place of a myriad tribal and ethnic groups; groups that are only united in sharing a belief in some form of Islam and a suspicious mistrust of all other Afghan groups; a mistrust that is exceeded only by a gut-level, intense suspicion of all non-Afghans. At the same time, all Afghans are governed by a code of Islamic hospitality towards strangers that makes them formally polite on first encounter but doesn't preclude later bumping them off.

Many of the men I saw were strikingly confident looking, even the most ugly or disfigured. Almost all had a warrior bearing. On our first day in Herat, a man told me proudly, "If you judge a place by the quality of the men, Afghanistan is a great place."

Commenting about our initial or subsequent impressions of female Afghans is difficult. Opportunities to view Afghan women were severely restricted. To speak with a lone woman was out of the question.

Even in 1971, before the Taliban attempted to drive all Afghan women back into the Middle Ages, many of the women were mobile human shapes covered in black from head to toe, walking tents with eye slits, with a stiff, raised-cloth beak over the nose and a mesh-covered opening over the mouth. Each tent contained a female human, but of what age or appearance, only her husband or close family could know.

Younger women in the cities or among the nomadic tribes were usually unveiled, but even a culturally insensitive type like me knew that for a strange man, infidel or not, to gaze for more than an accidental second, lustfully or otherwise, upon an Afghan woman was a serious no-no. There were never that many women out and about either, and then always in pairs or in little groups. A single woman could not go out on her own, except perhaps to walk to work in central Kabul.

Of course, Afghan women themselves through the centuries have been known to do horrible things to foreign military stragglers or to wounded tribal enemies. Afghan women are potentially dangerous in a number of ways.

Just listing some of the Afghan ethnic groups suggests the diversity of Afghan society: Hazaras, Tajiks, Baluchis, Pashtun (or Pushtun), Uzbeks, Nuristanis, and Turkmen. Though all shared some form of Islamic belief, they had little in common otherwise. And under each ethnic group, there were numerous actual tribes or informal family clans, headed up by a strong man.

Historically, and regardless of ethnicity, most Afghan groups enjoyed warfare: bashing each other and stealing their foes' goats and sheep, satisfying a taste for rape and pillage. Only one thing was certain to divert these warriors from their fondness for fighting with each other: the arrival of a foreign army. Killing infidel soldiers was better sport. It didn't create blood feuds with the neighboring clans. Plus, it put you right with Allah.

For a long time, Afghanistan had a Pashtun king who served more as a "first among equals" tribal chief than as the ruler of anything that could be called a country. At times the king's authority didn't stretch beyond Kabul or his own tribal area. The king could, however, summon a loya jirga, an advisory gathering of all the tribal groups that could, in turn, convey authority to make war, sign treaties, and so on.

Afghanistan is large country about the size of Texas and smack in the middle of Asia. All the historic east–west routes run across it. All roads go through Herat, a much-invaded city. From Herat, you can go north via Mazar e Sharif or straight through the middle, which involves high mountains and roads no better in places than dirt tracks, or south on a fairly good road that skirts the mountains in the center and goes via Kandahar. All these roads lead to Kabul and on to the Khyber Pass. If you want to invade India without crossing some of the world's highest mountains or most extreme deserts, the Khyber Pass is the only way to go.

Herat was a city with plenty of ruins, featuring precarious-looking, free-standing minarets of elegant beauty and semi-ruined mosques. There was a large, crumbling castle above the bazaar and the old town. I found Jane and Shelby without difficulty. We spent a while pottering in the bazaar, drinking tea in a tea house, and chatting with the local people—pointless, enjoyable stuff.

There were parks full of pine trees and children running around. Herat seemed like a pleasant place. Unfortunately, Jane and Shelby had explored it to their satisfaction while waiting for me. They wanted to press on. Reluctantly, I agreed. Like the hippies, we moved on in impulsive spurts.

We drove on fast to Kandahar. The US-built road was good, and gasoline was cheap. The southwest of Afghanistan, between Herat and Kandahar, is a dust-brown, high, arid plateau with occasional views of higher hills and of mountains to the north. Apart from the necessity of keeping an eye out for sheep and goats, the driving was easy.

Boys in Afghan Desert 1971

Kandahar struck all of us as a dangerous dump, though it was the scene of one of the few outright victories ever gained by a modern foreign army in Afghanistan. After a typical British colonial military disaster in mid-1880, the remains of the once-sizable British force retreated to the citadel in Kandahar and were besieged by one Ayub Khan. Since taking prisoners was never a key military objective for Afghans of whatever ethnic group, the outlook for these surrounded British and Indian soldiers wasn't promising.

In the agonizing heat of an Afghan August, General Roberts, the British commander-in-chief, force-marched ten thousand troops more than three hundred miles from Kabul to Kandahar. Roberts thrashed Ayub Khan outside Kandahar on September 1, 1880. General Roberts became Lord Roberts of Kandahar and the only general since Alexander who emerged from an Afghan campaign with an improved military reputation.

In Kabul, Lord Roberts avenged the brutal murder of the British representative in Kabul with the brisk public hanging of one hundred

Afghans on a spot facing the place the envoy was killed. Thus ended the Second Anglo-Afghan War. The Afghans were so subdued that the Third Anglo-Afghan War didn't occur until 1919.

Bearing in mind that the First Anglo-Afghan War had ended in 1842 with one, sole male British survivor from an army of twelve thousand, it is rash to criticize Lord Roberts' methods. Also, the Afghan women's practice of castrating British prisoners before killing them caused resentment. To show, though, that only punishment was intended, Lord Roberts left Afghanistan immediately after his success. This was a true act of wisdom.

I celebrated this rare British success with a hashish evening. To quote my journal:

In Kandahar I blew my mind. No other way to describe it. All the good dreams and all the bad dreams at once. Humbling. Erotic. Burning drought in throat. I had to lie down, then enjoyed it more and more until I awoke, sober and vaguely disappointed at about four in the morning. But more than eager to try it again.

Before leaving Kandahar, I had to go to a bank. The teller there told me in a near whisper what life in Kandahar was like for him. He had been educated abroad, and then came back, which he now bitterly regretted. He had spent time in prison; he had a large family, no money, no passport, and no prospects, but plenty of fear. By day he carried a knife, by night a pistol, since there were plenty of people in Kandahar who would kill him for a 1000 afghani (about fifteen to twenty dollars).

I was glad to leave Kandahar. Though the city is the key to controlling Afghanistan and the citadel is certainly impressive, it is a depressing, dangerous place.

By now we were going in a convoy, stopping at the same places. Jane rode with Friede in his VW, while I got Shelby. Shelby and I were still speaking—just—probably because Shelby was so upset about the Jane and Friede thing that she wanted someone to talk with about it. Given Jane's usual indifference to men, neither of us could understand how Jane and Friede had become an item so fast.

We drove through harsh, barren country, but we saw some irrigated farmland to the south. The concrete paved road was excellent. It was built by the Americans to outdo the Russians who had built a similar road from Kabul to the Soviet border via Mazar-e Sharif. The imperial competition that spawned the Great Game was alive and well.

Kabul was a scraggy, messy place among yet more barren hills, with a massive fortress, the Bala Hassar, dominating the town. A haze of pollution and wood smoke covered Kabul, even in summer. Shelby and I arrived ahead of Jane and Friede, so we went to find some spaghetti, which I suddenly craved.

While sitting in an Afghan hippie trattoria, I fell into conversation with a large, blond American sporting a Jesus hairstyle. When I mentioned to this friendly guy my newfound enthusiasm for hashish, he insisted at once that I must try smoking it in the Indian chellum his new best friend had. The friend would be most delighted, even overjoyed, to demonstrate his smoking technique, using this wonderful and ancient Indian invention.

The American and I rushed off together, leaving Shelby to think morose Ulster Protestant thoughts. He led me down a maze of side streets into a truly squalid guest house. We burst into the room of his friend. Oddly enough, the friend, a Frenchman, actually was delighted to see us, though the French girl whom he was mounting doggy-style in the middle of the room certainly was not. He swiftly dismounted. She pulled up her jeans and struck a pose of what was meant, I suppose, to be elegant Parisian disdain but only made her look petulant. The Frenchman started to prepare the pipe, pushing a cat and her kittens and an unspeakably revolting homemade litter box out of the way. The mess was bad but the smell was worse. Adding to it were many half-filled glasses of murky liquids and jars of Afghan yoghurt in various stages of secondary fermentation.

Nevertheless, I was thrilled by the scene, whatever the odor. I'd spent a few louche evenings in Saigon during my year in Vietnam, but that wasn't the same. There had been too many crazy GIs with shaved heads. I'd missed the sixties scene and wanted to catch up. Smoking hash with a French hippie? Color me Sartre.

We sat on the floor. The Frenchman fired up the chellum, which is a hollow brass hourglass with a damp cloth over one end and hashish in the other. Held correctly, you put your fingers over the cloth end and suck through your fingers so that your lips don't touch the pipe. Bob Dylan was on the cassette recorder, and the French girl brought out peaches in a bowl of water. This was what I had missed out on in San Francisco by going into the army in 1963. Time passed dreamily. Finally, the French girl rammed some scented salve up my nose to clear my head. I woozily left.

In Kabul, I soon discovered the money bazaar. Every morning in one section of the main bazaar, the day's exchange rate for the afghani, the local currency, was set. Intrinsically, the afghani had no value. You couldn't spend afghanis anyplace but Afghanistan. No one wanted the wads of dirty little notes, really, but it was convenient not to try to do every small transaction in dollars or pounds or rupees.

So, every morning in the bazaar, through much haggling, the money merchants would decide among themselves how many afghanis a dollar or a pound or a rupee would buy. All the money merchants agreed to the same exchange rate so that you could not arbitrage one against the other. The same process worked for gold, with the difference that the merchants set the price by listening to the BBC on transistor radios and finding out the gold price fix in London.

I was enjoying Kabul but, after a couple of days, Jane informed me that we were all going to Bamiyan and then on to Band-e-Amir, bang in the wild, high center of the country. Though hippies professed interest in exotic people and places, both hippies and pseudo-hippies like us actually moved around to be with other groups of hippies. So we dutifully set out on terrible dirt roads and ascended a 3000 meter pass to reach Bamiyan.

On arrival in Bamiyan, I wrote in my journal on July 31:

Into the delectable mountains. One hundred and twenty miles of broken-surfaced tracks through more and more beautiful river valleys, then into the great valley of Bamiyan. Fertile, irrigated, eight thousand feet high with the mighty mountains of the Hindu Kush on both sides of the valley.

Red forts, troglodyte dwellings and, on the north side, the greater and lesser Buddhas. So cold at night we needed blankets. We are even all getting along well!

Woke this morning to find the Honourable Jane cleaning the VW's air filter. What a woman! Jane then set off to see the Buddhas, and we followed at various intervals. Shelby and I climbed the great Buddha, then trotted along to the smaller one. Found Jane there perched in a hole about fifty feet up the Buddha. She explained that an attack of vertigo had left her there.

I came back in a mood of exhilaration to gorge on melons. Later I intend to ride (there were ponies to rent), then eat, then trip. The people in Bamiyan are handsome and friendly. Food is muck, as is the wine…" (Yes, there was local wine in pre-Taliban Afghanistan.) *"But no one cares a damn. The climate here is like wine.*

Shelby was in a filthy mood, nonetheless. Watching Jane go off to sleep with Friede in his VW wasn't fun for Shelby. Also she may have had a touch of altitude sickness. To fight this, Friede gave Shelby some speed. Since the speed kept Shelby up all night and she had a recurrence of dysentery, it was hard for her to answer the next morning whether it had helped with the altitude sickness.

On August 1, we drove to Band-e-Amir, along another thirty miles or so of broken road, up and over a 3500 meter pass into the heart of central Afghanistan and into another magnificent valley. The drive was challenging; the road was one lane and alarming; there were large fallen rocks, tight switchbacks, and unexpected drop-offs.

Band-e-Amir is one of the wonder spots on Earth. It features a remarkable series of large lakes. The middle sections of a descending sequence of massive limestone terraces had eroded in such a way that natural dams were created, forming a descending sequence of lakes with the deepest, most weirdly blue, perfectly clear, and agonizingly cold water in them. The lakes were large, but there were no signs of life in or around them. No boats. No weeds. Just the coldest, deepest, purest, bluish-green water I have ever seen. Because the lakes were formed by fairly recent erosion, the sides of the lakes were steep, bare banks or even rock cliffs.

Jane and Friede found a trail down to the dam holding back one of the upper lakes, a trail that filled me with fear as I worked my way down it with a heavy rucksack, several sleeping bags, and a complaining, jealous Shelby. The path was narrow, about two feet at the widest, and wormed along the side of a treeless, rocky, very steep mountain side. To fall off the path was to tumble hundreds of feet down into the deep icy waters of the lake. There were not even bushes to snatch at if you fell, only clumps of dry grass.

The natural dam was fairly flat on top and supported a variety of low bushes and small trees. A number of hippies were already installed on it, but there was plenty of free space. From the outside face of the dam, cascades of water emerged through fissures in the limestone. Blissfully, there were few insects, stinging or otherwise.

After some argument about where to camp (about which I was totally wrong, choosing a clearing in the middle of the path to the latrine), we agreed on a fairly sheltered spot in the center of the dam. By then it was five o'clock and already getting cold. I cut a good deal of brush for a fire, then made dinner for Friede and myself. Jane and Shelby were not eating for radically different reasons. I also made four hashish joints.

The ensuing trip was terrific but, in the middle of the now-familiar pink and yellow visions from *Dumbo* and *Fantasia*, I realized yet again that I was missing Alyson in an agonizingly erotic way. And that I would never love anyone else.

"Oh Alyson, Alyson," I thought, "If we are ever together again, I will never leave you."

In the morning I had to climb back to the VW for supplies. The climb was even more frightening than the descent the day before because I took a wrong turn. I found myself below the correct path on a lower track made by animals that came to a dead end. That meant clambering up on hands and knees to the right path since turning back was too tedious to consider. At over nine thousand feet, climbing on hands and knees was harder and no less nerve wracking than the subsequent hike down from the top.

We met two fun Frenchmen, Robert and Andre, who joined our gang. They were younger than I and on holiday from the Ecole Polytechnique.

Robert and Andre immediately freaked us out with a horrid rumor they had picked up in some French embassy. (As Polytechniciens, Robert and Andre travelled effortlessly from French embassy to French embassy, where they were housed, wined, and dined.)

According to the rumor, the Club Mediterranee was going to build a large Club Med on the most beautiful of all the lakes, the Sword Lake. We must see this wonder before we left. Unfortunately no one was certain exactly where the Sword Lake was or even how to tell which lake it was.

The charming names of the lakes at Band-i-Amir are Cheese, Mint, Slaves, Sword, and Awe. We were pretty sure that we were camping on the Mint Lake, but our maps were rudimentary. Robert and Andre said that they would guide us to the Sword Lake through the sheer force of their trained Gallic intellects. To show our commitment to the search, we all first went swimming. The cold water reduced our testicles to the size and texture of frozen peas.

First, we tried to climb to the Sword Lake on foot but failed to catch even a glimpse of it before reaching terrain that required mountain-climbing kit to ascend any further. We then tried going up two different tracks in the VW. Even with Robert and Andre standing on the rear bumper of the VW for extra traction, Elsie could not go up either track. (We were consoled to learn that a Land Rover had failed in the same way the day before.) We tried to find Sword Lake by attempting to drive around our lake to the other side but again failed. The Frenchmen were in great spirits and found the quest hysterically funny. They began debating in Franglais as to which of the English speakers carried the most varieties of bowel remedy.

The next day effectively ended the hippie phase of my trip. The day started slowly, with me noting in my journal, "Today is certainly the fourth of August, so I will have to decide where the third went someday." The lakes were just as stunning, the sky just as intensely blue, the air just as intoxicating. We had enough dried soup and pasta to stay at Band-e-Amir indefinitely.

I had realized that Jane and Friede were cooking up some kind of adventure but was still surprised when they arrived late morning mounted on two scraggy ponies. The ponies were fitted out with crude Afghan saddles over pieces of maroon carpet and simple rope bits, and they were fully loaded for a trip. (Today a New York interior decorator would pay thousands for the saddles and carpets. Even with the smell.)

Jane and Friede were going off for a jaunt with some tribal horsemen they had met who were willing to accept the Honourable Jane as an honorary man. (By then she was so thin that with her short, messy hair she looked like a school boy with advanced TB.) The horsemen were kuchis, nomadic Pashtun tribesmen who are mistrusted by settled Afghans. I knew Jane too well and respected her too much to comment on her plan. Friede was a doctor and competent in all sorts of ways. I felt that they would survive. I shook hands with Friede and simply said "have fun and take care" to Jane.

Shelby immediately threw a mega-wobbly. She wept, demanding that the VW be unloaded and all of Jane's kit removed and left behind. Fortunately Andre, whom Shelby respected, told her not to be silly. I thought, "Not just silly – a silly cow!" and was immediately ashamed of my feelings. I knew that Shelby loved Jane and wanted to protect her. I also knew that Shelby had terrible gut-rot, which made all of us at various times feel like crying. But we were bold, independent adults. For Jane to go off with Friede and the tribal horsemen might be Jane's great adventure. This was *The Wilder Shores of Love*.

After this upheaval, staying on at Band-e-Amir was less appealing. The next day Shelby, Andre, Robert, and I set off to drive back to Kabul via a different route. This involved using what the map showed as a proper road. This road should eventually take us back to the main Russian-built highway linking Kabul and Mazar-e-Sharif. We should hit the paved road at Dowshi, fifty miles or so north of Kabul, and north of the mighty Salang Pass. This would be an exciting drive.

The distance to Dowshi was as unclear as the map itself. Road maps of interior Afghanistan then were more an indication of possibilities than an accurate guide. Bridges could be marked that were actually washed out but crudely and usably repaired with logs; stretches of track washed away; large boulders dropped from high on the mountain side right into the middle of the track. We would encounter all these things.

From the start, there was the terrain itself to awe us. It was arid, brutal, rocky, empty, and thrilling. Multiple shades of brown slid into each other as the sun moved across the mountains. If you have seen the Superstition Mountains in Arizona or the Sierra Nevada, you will have an idea of the terrain in the central parts of Afghanistan. Getting lost was unwise. We had jerry cans of water but only enough for a few days in the heat.

The driving was painfully slow and trying, yet interesting at the same time. We picked our way up the side of one dry canyon and made our way over a ridge, only to find ourselves in another canyon, for hour after hour. Apart from the occasional hawk or vulture, there was no life and no greenery. Try to imagine the most glorious, spectacular, utterly dry mountain scenery. There were no road signs, no truck stops, no people—no nothing. When we stopped for a break or to move large rocks out of the road, we spontaneously shouted with joy.

O, Afghanistan! What a wonder you were!

Even with the most careful driving and frequent stops to examine the track ahead, by that afternoon we had broken two and possibly all four shock absorbers, snapped the cable from the accelerator pedal to the engine, and permanently turned the VW's heating on. The last was not unbearable, even in August, since the heating in Elsie was totally ineffectual. But the accelerator cable problem was serious. We were stuck.

We were high up an isolated gorge, stopped in the middle of the rutted track. There were steep hills on both sides and a dry stream beside the road. We had seen no one for hours. At this point I discovered why graduates of the Ecole Polytechnique run France. I got out the toolbox. Andre and Robert scrounged through it. Shelby supplied a number of hair pins. Andre, who was slender, lay on his back and pulled himself under the VW. Robert stood by and responded to Andre's muffled shouts and curses from underneath: *Merde alors! Putain de machine! Donnez-moi les pinces. Merde, merde, merde!*

I was standing by Elsie, wondering if Andre could make the VW drivable, when I noticed a man walking down the track toward us. He was only fifty feet away by the time I spotted him. He wore a dirty turban and some sort of fur-trimmed cloak and had a rifle over his shoulder—an old but effective-looking bolt-action rifle. Our only weapon was a Swiss Army knife. Andre and Robert couldn't see the man approaching. Bandits were not unknown in Afghanistan. Our stuff would represent a fortune to a rural Afghan. We, on the other hand, were worth less than nothing, dead or alive. Shouting was pointless or worse; it might spur him into action.

The man came up to me. He smiled, displaying his remaining two or three yellow teeth, and pulled his cloak open. Hanging inside it were half a dozen freshly killed rabbits. The guy was a peaceful, friendly hunter who wanted to show us how successful he had been and to sell us a rabbit. Andre climbed out from under Elsie, having fixed the accelerator cable with wire and hairpins. We bought a rabbit, and the man wandered off. By then it was getting dark, and we camped by the side of the road.

That night Andre and Robert skinned and ate the rabbit. I watched them eat under a very starry night sky. There was no light anywhere beyond our camp. It was a place of holy wonder, but I missed Alyson horribly. By Camping Gaz lantern I wrote: "I will be shattered if she finds Mr. Right while I am away. More fool I."

The next morning we limped back to Kabul the way we had come, backtracking all the way. We could only go ten miles per hour. The VW bounced and rolled about on the broken shocks.

In Kabul, I found a proper, factory-authorized VW garage, Kabul Automobile, run by two chubby, cheerful Afghan brothers who had been trained at Wolfsburg in Germany. We chatted – me in my US Army pidgin German. They told me to replace all the Stossdampferen with oversize Boge export-special shock absorbers. Otherwise, Elsie needed only a new accelerator cable and the heating valve replaced.

While I was waiting for the work to be done, a brand new VW engine was hauled in on an ox cart, straight from Kabul airport. The brothers told me they could get almost any VW part within forty-eight hours. Such attention to logistics took Hitler's Wehrmacht, driving the jeep-like ancestor of Elsie, to the outskirts of Moscow.

Shelby and I agreed to part company in Kabul, although I agreed to carry most of her stuff plus Jane's to India. We arranged a place to meet in India. I went by myself that night to the Bost Restaurant. This eatery is mentioned in the 1971 edition of Nancy Hatch Dupree's *An Historical Guide to Kabul*, a quirky, useful book that I only discovered years later.

I was eating my usual kebab when an American guy of about fifty spoke to me. He didn't want to drink by himself, he said, and ordered me a Czech pilsner beer. Looking like a New England prep school housemaster complete with round, horn-rimmed glasses, and with a name like Frank O'Toole, he had obviously already been drinking heavily.

Frank claimed to be a top man at the US embassy, and I believed him. Probably Frank was the CIA head; there was something tweedy and Ivy League about him like the CIA types I'd met before. I was filthy dirty, so when Frank suggested that I go back to his flat with him and use his shower which had actual running hot water, I accepted at once.

After my shower, we drank beer with shots of aquavit. Frank had pictures of his four sons on the walls. We played a dice game for a while. I had wondered if Frank was gay when he poked his head in to look at me in the shower but then assumed otherwise when he talked about his sons. He spoke in a slow, maudlin way as he drank. This was a most unhappy fellow.

I was thinking about leaving when Frank made his pitch. "We could make each other so happy," Frank said. My initial instinct had been correct. I told Frank firmly that I was hopelessly and incurably heterosexual and then ignorantly and tactlessly asked him if he had ever talked to anyone about his unhappiness. Frank muttered, "No analysis," and told me to leave. Which I was glad to do since he was weeping.

Driving eastwards out of Kabul towards Jalalabad reminded me of *Flashman*, by George MacDonald Fraser, a howlingly funny novel. That the subject matter involves the catastrophic British defeat in the First Anglo-Afghan War doesn't mar the comedy. Flashman is a cowardly anti-hero who becomes a full-blown military hero despite despicable behavior, lying, and avoiding combat whenever possible. Such tactics would have been needed in spades to survive the total massacre of the actual British colonial expeditionary force in 1842.

Field Marshal Sir Gerald Templar, who defeated the Communists in Malaya, refers to the retreat from Kabul as "the most disgraceful and humiliating episode in our history of war against an Asian enemy up to that time."

Some twelve thousand soldiers, of whom four thousand five hundred were British soldiers, marched up to Kabul from the Indian Punjab in 1841. On January 13, 1842, the guards at the British fort in Jalalabad saw a single horseman approaching them. This was Dr. Brydon, the only British soldier to survive. Apart, of course, from the fictional Harry Flashman.

Driving down this road, I saw exactly what happened to the British forces once the insane decision was made, abandon Kabul in winter. Ravine followed crag; crag followed ravine; the road was exposed to fire from above on all sides. Afghans were—and are—excellent rifle shots at long distances. Picking off stragglers from the main force was another of their specialties. And then the Afghan women fell upon the wounded at night, finished them off and robbed the corpses.

Overall, Afghanistan is one of the most unpromising places on earth for a foreign army to invade, right up there with the vastnesses of Russia and the jungle hills of Vietnam. The Afghans stopped Alexander the Great and the British Empire in its prime and would help finish off the Soviet Union. None of these would-be conquerors were hobbled by habeas corpus or international law. And none of them gave a damn about democracy, fair elections, or nation building. But they all failed anyway.

Bouncing along in Elsie at thirty-five miles per hour, these were matters for future reflection. The heat and dust were horrible but now seemed normal. Andre and Robert were still with me. We made our way down the Khyber Pass, past many forts and checkpoints, and down switchback after switchback. It was a long descent down through rugged hills.

That evening we stopped in Peshawar, Pakistan, whose dominant inhabitants are Pashtuns, or Pathans, as the British called them. Pashtuns are also the dominant tribe in southeastern Afghanistan, so Peshawar has a tribal Afghan feel to it. We walked past many gun makers in small, open-fronted shops, who were making good copies of old British military weapons. I tried the bolt action on one. Smooth as butter.

We went to a film. Many in the audience brought their rifles in with them. There was no nonsense about checking guns at the door. Appropriately, the feature film was *A Fistful of Dollars*. Before the feature, a newsreel was shown about the recent Pakistani attack on East Bengal, then a part of Pakistan and now the independent Bangladesh. Millions of refugees had fled into India. Hundreds of thousands of miserably poor civilian Bengali Muslims had died. Here in Peshawar, their equally miserably poor Muslim brothers cheered at the horrors in the newsreel. War was in their blood. I half-expected them to let off their rifles in the cinema. Later, sporadic gunfire went on through the night.

Driving to Lahore was slow and laborious but interesting. We left the arid country and entered the subtropics. The road was tied up with a mixture of military traffic and bullock carts. It was also narrow, so constant attention was needed even to creep along. Vultures fed on good-sized animal carcasses by the roadside. In Lahore, apart from staying in an absolute dump, I was thrilled to be in the world of my literary hero, Kipling, whose masterpiece, *Kim*, begins with Kim as a young boy in Lahore climbing on the great cannon, Zam-Zammah:

He sat, in defiance of municipal orders, astride the gun Zam-Zammah on her brick platform opposite the old Ajaib-Gher—the Wonder House, as the natives call the Lahore Museum. Who hold Zam-Zammah, that 'fire-breathing dragon', hold the Punjab, for the great green-bronze piece is always first of the conqueror's loot.

Kipling's father was in charge of the Lahore Museum. Kipling came to Lahore in 1882 to work on the *Civil and Military Gazette*.

I spent some time outside the museum, looking at this enormous cannon, some fifteen feet long and with the wheels on the gun carriage the height of a man, while thinking about Kipling and the lost colonial world he immortalized. The humid heat got to me, so I retreated to a Chinese restaurant that boasted air conditioning. After that, I returned to Kipling's world by going to an old British hotel with wood paneling, waiters in white outfits, and ceiling fans. I had several beers on the veranda.

There was no letter from Alyson in Lahore. Damn!

I drove down the high road into India, through some of the best farmland in the world. Families supported themselves well on small plots. People looked healthy. The men—Jats—were big and muscular. Stopping overnight in Chandigarh, we arrived in Delhi on August 13.

Delhi made a magnificent first impression. It is enormous and teems with life. The celebrated Red Fort is indeed red and also vast; the great mosque, the Jama Masjid, is splendid. It is next to the Chandi Chowk, the main bazaar. Delhi was the capitol of the Mughal Empire prior to the British conquest of India. The British capital was Calcutta until it was moved to Delhi in 1911. Many cities existed on and around the location of today's Delhi; the area is a treasure trove of lost and ruined cities.

New Delhi, created from a plan by the English architect, Lutyens, was originally a suitably grand capital of the Indian Empire, with massive colonnaded buildings all in white, broad avenues, and grand squares. Sadly, the New Delhi of 1971 was neglected, shabby and dirty. The charm of Delhi was further diminished by unusually pungent smells, reflecting many, many blocked drains. There were crows and vultures picking at rubbish everywhere.

Also marring my initial impression was my first exposure to the Indian habit of crapping behind bus-stop shelters. Yes, I am aware of the shortage of public toilets in India. However, central London has few free pit stops. Yet even Brits in the most urgent need don't relieve themselves behind the nearest bus stop, do they?

Finding a hotel was frustrating too. I was spoiled. On our way to India, after camping became too dangerous, we usually stayed in dumps and hovels, but they were cheap and easy to find. In Delhi, the French guys and I went first to the YMCA. The Y was clean but wanted about two dollars apiece per night, a fortune compared to what we had been paying.

A seemingly helpful young Sikh on a Lambretta offered to guide us to a cheaper hotel. Hopping back in the VW, we followed this guy through the traffic of one of the world's largest and busiest cities for about a half hour before we realized that he was taking us to some relative's house far out in the sticks. I persuaded him with some difficulty to take us back to the Y, where we stayed. But whatever the chaos, heat and smells, I loved Delhi as a whole.

Wandering around the streets near the YMCA, I met a delightful old Sikh, gloriously bearded, mustached, and turbaned, who owned and operated an Indianoil petrol station but whose real joy in life had been as a Subadur-Major (like the regimental sergeant major in the British Army) in the Indian Army under the British. He joined the Indian Army in 1936, fought in the war, and was the first of many Sikhs to ask me when the British were coming back. To have said never would have been cruel, so I asked him about the chances of India going to war with Pakistan. He thought that the Indian diplomatic pact with Russia lessened its chances.

War with Pakistan didn't concern the old soldier. He thought that the Pakistanis in the west were good fighters but did not maintain their equipment properly. Unfortunately, the Americans had recently resupplied the Pakistanis, he said. This, however, could only delay their inevitable defeat. The old man took me for a Brit, and I did not correct him. Like all true Sikhs, one of his names was Singh, but sadly I have lost his full name.

A true Sikh wears a sacred bangle, does not cut his hair, and carries a knife. They are a warrior people and heavily represented in the modern Indian military as pilots, paratroopers, tank commanders, and so forth. Sikhs also provide some of the world's most insanely brave and most dangerous truck drivers. Whenever I faced one of these grinning, turbaned, warrior drivers behind the wheel of a massive Tata truck, driving like a go-kart racer right down the high-crowned middle of a narrow Indian road, I always instantly gave way.

My Family—Who Art in Cleveland

I went to Connaught Place, the commercial center of New Delhi, to the American Express office where I hoped to find some money. No money there but some letters. One was from Alyson; it was an instant source of joy.

The other letter, from my parents, was a source of instant irritation. They insisted that I return from India to Cleveland, Ohio, for the wedding of my sister. I missed the wedding of my brother by being in the US Army in Vietnam. War was a reasonable excuse for missing a family wedding. Being in India was not. My parents would pay me back for the ticket. The wedding was in a week, and I was expected.

Damn! I'd known about a possible wedding, but since I also knew plenty about the groom-to-be, I'd hoped that somehow it wouldn't happen. Damn! I decided that my sister, however nutty, deserved the support of her elder brother on what was likely to be a bad, bad day for her. There are no universal rules for a happy marriage, but "Never marry a Greek" isn't a bad one for a start.

Connaught Place, like the rest of New Delhi, had seen better days, but it hummed commercially. The framework of the white-columned grandeur that Lutyens had planned was still there somewhere under the cracking facades and movie posters. I discovered that there was no way I could afford even a one-way air ticket bought legitimately. But I soon discovered that there were much cheaper options.

In 1971, India was still in the grip of the British-style bureaucratic socialism beloved by Nehru. There were elaborate controls on currency movements, for example. The value of the rupee was kept artificially high against the dollar and European currencies. There were controls and high, protective tariffs on all sorts of imports, so that even a used pair of underpants or a bra from Marks and Spencer in the UK could be sold at a nice profit. Real Swiss watches were particularly hot stuff.

I decided not to flog my Omega wristwatch yet. In a short space of time I sold the Blaupunkt radio out of the VW, changed the Deutschemarks I carried in a sewn-in pouch at my waist for rupees at a favorable rate of exchange (after checking the official rate in American Express), and found a slippery travel agent who would sell me a ticket to the States via London for a fraction of the listed price. The ticket looked valid, and so it turned out to be, but not without a few little quirks, like many stops and putting me on Alitalia for much of the way.

I then went to a post office and sent Alyson a telegram, asking her to meet me in London. There was no way that she could get back to me, so I would just have to hope that she received the telegram and wanted to see me. Her few letters were warm, but what reception would I get?

For the next couple of days, I lived it up with Andre and Robert. They arranged for me to join them for tea with the French ambassador to India. I cleaned myself up as best I could and followed my French pals into the splendors of the French embassy. The ambassador could only stay a minute but left us in the care of his wife and two busty, attractive daughters. Somehow my atrocious French was up to the occasion and I didn't overly embarrass myself.

Later we went out with the daughters. They took us to a Western disco called the Cellar. The two girls talked to glamorous Indian pals and ignored not just me but the two brilliant Polytechniciens. Something else did not ignore me; luckily Andre and Robert proposed leaving just before I would have had to leave in a spectacular hurry. I was beginning to wonder if I had some sort of long-lasting bowel bug. The earthquake or heroic phase of my immune system's struggle with this bastardly microbe had begun and more-or-less ended in Shiraz, but drastic aftershocks continued.

On the long flight to London, I read V.S. Naipul's *An Area of Darkness*. Naipul, of Indian origin but from Trinidad, writes in this somber, scornful book about the shock and disappointment of his first trip to India. Cruelty, filth, and religious hypocrisy are rammed in the reader's face. I reacted with disgust at Naipul. All of those things are to be found in India, but so are all the wonders of the human race and beauty on an epic scale. To see only the horrors of India without seeing the glories is to be a pathetic, sneering fool.

Phoning Alyson upon arrival, I was happy beyond bounds to find that she was indeed waiting to see me. I went to the New Theatre in

London's West End, where she worked. Alyson came down the stairs in what I called her "skirt of many colors," in red, brown, and blue. She was doing some modeling in it.

I had forgotten how tall she was and how thick and beautiful her long dark hair was. We went to the Salisbury, an old Edwardian pub next to the New Theatre, and talked and talked, then went to Battersea Park, lay on the grass and talked some more. I was enchanted to be with Alyson and physically lustful. That night we made uncomplicated, joyous love repeatedly.

In the morning I had to rush to Heathrow for the next leg of my flight. Before I left her flat, we talked about the future, which worried both of us. This was now something serious. Alyson said that she was frightened that I would hurt her and that I was sometimes painfully offhand. My feelings weren't offhand, I said. But what would happen to us next?

For me, Cleveland happened next. Every time I went back to my parent's house, I expected something to be different. But just as Cleveland continued to decay, my ever-dysfunctional family degenerated along with our fair city. I arrived with a fever and gut-rot. My parents were caught up with the wedding, happily, and didn't bother me at first. After discovering on the bathroom scale that I had lost over twenty pounds since the trip started, I went to bed in a deluge of sweat.

I woke to find my mother in a long white nightgown, very drunk, standing over me like someone auditioning for the part of Lady Macbeth, and shouting that I must get out of bed and change my dripping-wet T-shirt. I did so and went off for another session on the loo. When I came back, I found that mother had pulled the bedding off the bed, and then found herself too drunk to remake it with dry sheets.

Enter my feisty younger brother, Maynard. He abrasively told my mother to go to bed. She responded by telling him that he was behaving like a Jew. (My brother's wonderful wife is Jewish.) This caused my brother to speculate loudly about the pleasures of punching female drunkards in the mouth.

At this point, having finished remaking the bed, I made them both leave. The last thing I heard before falling off to sleep again was my mother screaming hoarsely and drunkenly for my father to come upstairs. She wanted a sympathetic drinking companion.

By the following day, my fever was gone and my bowels had resumed – temporarily - their normal rate of activity. A full emotional and physical recovery, though, meant getting the hell out of Cleveland and far away from my family—fast.

I called Alyson and asked her to fly back to India with me. She said yes! I rushed out and somehow organized enough money for us to fly from London to Dehli together.

Drink and smoking grass got me through the rest of the wedding fiasco. The groom, Stavros, was more loathsome than any husband I'd imagined even my totally ditzy sister selecting. With his deep, Greek-accented voice, his John Lennon hairstyle and round, steel-framed glasses, there was an ominous, horror-film air about Stavros. This fit right into our Addams Family scene. On August 31 I wrote: "Out of this private funny farm; back to England, Alyson, and India. Oh joy!"

My reunion with Alyson in London was blissful. Alyson's beautiful mother was staying with her. I warmed to Josephine at once since she didn't question my sleeping with Alyson or the fact that I, a strange, haggard-looking, wild-haired American of no fixed abode was taking her number three daughter off to India. Perhaps that was due to Josephine having four other daughters? Or that Josephine was born in Egypt and the daughter of a senior British colonial officer? Perhaps "pay, pack and follow" was in her DNA.

To India with Alyson

E xcept for almost missing our flight, the trip back to India was uneventful. As before, Alyson had packed her pet rocks in the ancient leather suitcase, resulting in a weight so over the tourist-class allowance that anguished negotiations were needed. We were a little late at check-in anyway. Alyson showed no obvious signs of cold feet but somehow once at Heathrow and checked in, I couldn't get her to go to the gate. We arrived at the BOAC VC-10 just as the cabin crew was closing the door.

On the seventh of September, we arrived back in Delhi. I'd learned from our Venetian experience and booked us in at the Jan Path Hotel, which I'd checked out before leaving. It was cavernous and damp but cool and had proper beds and flush toilets. I didn't want India to hit Alyson too abruptly. I wanted her to love India as I did.

In the taxi on the way to the Jan Path, we ran into torrential monsoon rain. The rain splashed up through large rust holes in the floor of the Hindustan taxi. When Alyson commented to the driver that the monsoon should have ended, he replied, "No one can know the program of God."

I agreed with the driver; I was amazed and dazed and overjoyed that fate had linked Alyson with me. She on the other hand was tired, confused, and had the curse. We discovered that night that Alyson found sleeping a problem if there was the slightest noise or discomfort. Her fatigue became a challenge for both of us. That night I tried to cuddle her to sleep with no success.

Before we could set out on our travels, there was an urgent matter to deal with. During the long flight, I'd discovered that Alyson's homeopathic doctor, an Indian named Dr. Chandra Sharma, MD (failed) Bombay, had persuaded Alyson that no inoculations were needed to travel in India.

This was beyond insane; people with recent smallpox scars on their faces were everywhere, as were small children obviously crippled by polio. We found a clinic, and Alyson was shot full of every available vaccine. I watched to make sure new needles were used. This was the first of two horrid medical frights that I would have Dr. Sharma to thank for.

Alyson was shocked and thrilled by Delhi, as I had been. Women beggars pushed their starving babies at us as we walked past the alleyways they lived in. Boys slept on the pavement, oblivious to pedestrians. Families cooked their meals on the pavements - little yellow cakes fried in some kind of smelly oil. People were shitting and spitting everywhere: in front of smart shops, behind bus shelters, and next to government offices. A crippled beggar boy pushed himself along on an oven tray with casters. It had all the teeming humanity of a brilliantly colorful documentary film.

We retrieved Elsie the VW from a garage near the YMCA and set off for Agra, having dropped off Jane and Shelby's stuff. Jane was staying at the YMCA with no sign of Friede. Shelby and Jane appeared to be pals again. I resolved to get Jane alone and find out what had happened to the wild horsemen and Friede later. But I never did.

Driving in India requires intense concentration to avoid hitting loose and naked toddlers, ancient scrawny cows, or elderly people calmly chatting in the middle of narrow, two-lane roads. Malnourished bicyclists wobbled slowly and unpredictably from one side of the road to the other. Women road menders walked in and out of the traffic with baskets of stones on their heads. By the side of the road, there were ponds where buffalos wallowed. The varied greens and the sheer fertility of the rich soil were stunning. There were few road signs, and those were mostly confusing, except for the one which read, "Safety First, Luck Afterwards."

There were few private autos but many bullock carts. Stray nails from the steel shoes on the bullocks pulling the carts were scattered all over the roads and roadsides. These nails caused constant flat tires. When a flat occurred, the drill was always the same. I would unpack enough stuff to get at the spare tire and the jack, put on the spare, and drive into the nearest village.

Even tiny villages had a shop that hot patched tires. Squatting in the Asian way, the tire-wallah would pry the tube out of the tire and find the hole with a bucket of water and an air hose. Then a patch would be cut to shape, a smear of rubber cement would be put on it, and then the patch would be sealed on to the tube with a hot iron. Alyson and I would stand out of the sun under the village banyan tree and watch the process. Friendly, curious people would in turn gather to watch us.

Piles of tires too ruined to patch were made into sandals by the tire-wallah's sons. I finally found a pair of sandals that were big enough for my size 12 feet and still have them—somewhere. Alyson found the sandals a little crude and rejected my suggestions to buy a pair. The design was similar to the Ho Chi Minh Nike's I remembered from Vietnam.

Near one tire repair stop, we encountered a traditional snake charmer, dressed only in sandals and a loin cloth. He made a large, fine cobra come out of a narrow-necked wicker container by playing a wooden flute (I think it was the vibrations that motivated the snake), then asked me in sign language if we would like to see his mongoose kill a cobra? Alyson was appalled, but I haggled a price.

The snake charmer released the little mongoose, produced a different, smaller cobra and dropped it on the ground. This got the mongoose's full attention. We watched carefully as the little mongoose stood up on its hind legs, and the snake swayed its head. The mongoose swayed with the cobra.

Wham! We did not watch carefully enough. In one lightning-smooth move, the mongoose bit through the cobra's neck, just below its hood, and hung on for dear life. In a nanosecond the snake was on the ground in the dust, writhing in death. The snake charmer, though, was also quick and grabbed Rikki-Tikki-Tavi before he could eat the cobra. There was no trickery; the cobra still had its fangs and was killed fairly.

When we arrived in Agra and tried to stay at a funny, old European-style hotel that someone had recommended, the funny, old Hungarian woman who was the owner and desk clerk promptly asked us for a marriage license. So we left and stayed at a clean, simple Indian place, the Hotel Jaiwal. Our room was off a balcony over an interior courtyard that contained a cow and her calf. They mooed softly to each other while we spent the afternoon making love.

In a light rain as dusk was falling, we went to the Taj Mahal. Only a handful of people were there. We wandered by ourselves in the midst of hundreds of fireflies—little, creamy glowing points against the dimmer sheen of the white-marble mass of the Taj. Shah Jahan, the Mughal Emperor, built the Taj to commemorate the death in childbirth of Mumtaz Mahal, his favorite wife. She died giving birth to his fourteenth child in 1648. Her grave is in the center, right under the enormous marble onion dome, with his grave to the side. Inside the Taj, there was just enough light to see the exquisite inlaid jasper calligraphy, repeating over and over the name of Allah.

Walking outside in the mist, the glow of the Taj's white marble, even in the dusk, plus the fireflies, overwhelmed me. In the heavy, warm night air, there was an aroma of jasmine. I felt faint for an instant, then ravenously hungry.

Over a good meal, Alyson and I naturally talked about the nature of love. Love, for Alyson, was the greatest adventure. We joked about Kipling's stories of discreet-but-passionate affairs in Simla, the summer capital of the British Raj, and the havoc that Alyson could have created there. With dinner, I was offered a local brandy called Golconda. Despite the appealing name, I settled instead for some local whiskey. It was rough indeed.

Drinking in India in 1971 was often challenging. There were several excellent local beers, like Kingfisher, but there were complex and perverse Indian local or state rules about where beer could be sold. In some places you could carry it into a restaurant in a paper bag, then consume it openly. In others, the restaurant would send a boy out for a bottle that was not legal to consume openly, so you would place it on the floor next to your chair and slyly glug from it. There were local boozes purporting to be Scotch whiskey, London gin, and plain old rum. All were more or less the right color and certainly high in alcohol. The rum was the least unpleasant in taste.

In the morning we went back to the Taj. Again there were few tourists—perhaps a dozen. In 1971, India was completely off the global travel map. Air travel was relatively expensive in those days, but I believe the real reasons that kept the older or unadventurous Westerners away were: the well-publicized probability of war with Pakistan; bureaucratic bumbling by the Indian tourist authorities; few hotels of a Western standard (and even fewer with Western toilets); fears of seeing heart-rending poverty or, worse, of being murdered by the vengeful poor; and, finally, fears of catching some awful disease. These fears worked hugely to our benefit. That morning we wandered through the Taj Gardens hand in hand, largely on our own, shielding our eyes with our hands from the intense sunlight reflected off the white marble.

Later, down from our emotional high, we thought warmly of the icy Lord Curzon, greatest of all the British Viceroys of India, who restored the Taj in the 1890s and thus saved it for us.

The next evening we were introduced to a more Kiplingesque side of India. We stayed at Shivapuri on the main road to Bombay in a Dak bungalow. Dak bungalows were built at regular intervals along major roads by the British for the convenience of traveling officials. They were small, one-story hotels with a veranda around the building and a central corridor that ran from front to back with rooms off each side of the corridor. Like many things built by the British, who left India forever in 1947, this Dak bungalow had seen better days.

An old greybeard greeted us after I stood in the central corridor shouting for a while. "Of course you can have a room," he said. "You can have the best room." This large room had a low, wide bed. A small room next to it had a hole in the floor with several buckets of water next to it. No wash basin, no soap, and of course no loo paper.

The rooms once had whitewashed walls, but only traces of whitewash were left. The effect was of grey gloom under very high ceilings. The smell from the loo hole was penetrating. There was a ceiling fan that worked slowly and one electric light on the single table by the bed. There was a supply of candles, also on the table, but I had brought my Camping Gaz lantern in case the electricity failed in the night. The discarded matches around the candles made me think that this was likely.

There was no lock on the door. And there were holes in the walls so that someone in the next room could observe us. But the holes appeared to be merely the result of wear and tear rather than for the use of a voyeur. I stuffed rags into the larger ones. It was a creepy place.

Alyson accepted staying in the Dak bungalow remarkably calmly. Her grandfather had been in the British colonial service in Egypt; her mother was born in Egypt, and her father was a British officer in India during World War II, so some ancestral stoicism or genetic adaptability may have come into play. I tried to assure her that the place was perfectly safe. I cleaned around the loo hole with Jeyes Fluid, a powerful traditional British disinfectant. This cut the fruity richness of the smell a bit.

The greybeard told us that dinner would not be for a while, so I went out to explore. In the village near the Dak bungalow I met a chubby, pleasant man who was lying on a string bed, nursing a broken leg. We chatted. We established an interest in common; he wanted to buy certain items from me.

Though it was a simple village, he had plenty of cash. I sold him some of the Camping Gaz cylinders and all the underpants I could spare. I regretted having sold the VW radio but decided to hang on to my old Omega watch for a little while longer. I toyed with the idea of trying to sell some of Alyson's bras and knickers but decided against this. The Dak bungalow wasn't the right setting for suggesting this little transaction to Alyson.

Dinner was on the veranda at the back of the Dak bungalow. Night was falling. Jasmine grew aromatically all over the back of the bungalow. Attractive green lizards ran around above us on the ceiling of the veranda. The food wasn't bad either: an omelet, curried potatoes, rice, and chapattis. A romantic scene. We smiled fondly at each other. This was love.

Night fell with a jolt. Hard-to-identify noises and numerous flying insects appeared. The noises became louder. Suddenly, there was a lot of canine howling. The corridor running through the bungalow was full of scrabbling, snapping, and snarling. Two large male mongrels were in a violent fight. They burst through the screen door and out onto the veranda where we were eating. They ran past our table, knocked over a spare chair, and ran off howling into the night. Having heard horror stories about rabid dogs, we were both unpleasantly surprised by this. We immediately left the table and went to our room.

The surprises weren't over. We started getting ready for bed. Alyson went into the room with the hole in the floor. I was sitting on the edge of the low bed when Alyson shouted in horror. I rushed in. After a pee, Alyson had made the mistake of looking at the nasty hole in the floor. Ants and massive dung beetles were emerging from the hole in the floor to see what was available. I resisted the urge to step on the beetles, which, after all, were only doing what nature designed them to do.

Alyson stiffened her upper lip again in a splendidly British way. I wedged the only chair against the corridor door, which couldn't be locked. We settled down on the bed and started to think about sleep. However, there was a low noise in the hall. Alyson popped up, removed the chair, and looked out our door. Another shock. Two tough-looking men were lying asleep on the floor of the corridor right outside our door, snoring away on bamboo mats.

Since we were in the area where the legendary Thuggee stranglers had been active in the nineteenth century, and since we had discussed the Thuggee and their garroting technique that day while driving, Alyson was not pleased by this discovery. (The Thuggee were a secret, quasi-religious sect who specialized in murdering travelers by strangling them lightning fast with special knotted ropes. This satisfied some religious ritual need and was a nice little earner to boot.) We had also been warned not to travel at night, as there were modern dacoits, or bandits, along the way. I persuaded her that the men were probably long-distance truck drivers, peacefully bedded down for the night. This explanation may even have been true; the men were gone when we got up, safe and sound, the next morning.

For the next few days we drove slowly through the Ghats, a chain of hills that run roughly north to south in western India. We were heading for the celebrated Ajanta caves. The scenery was vividly green and lushly dramatic. As in Afghanistan, there were no road signs and no billboards, but here the climate was tropical and humid. Unlike sparsely populated Afghanistan, there were people and cows everywhere; on the road, on the hills, lying on the ground—everywhere. Men stood in little groups to watch the road, even though there was little traffic. They blew their noses frequently, using the old farmer method of blocking one nostril with a grubby finger and blowing the yucky out the other. Then they wiped the muck off with the back of a hand. And then they spat.

One day as we drove, Alyson demanded a medal.
"A medal?" I exclaimed. "What medal?"
"The VC," Alyson replied. "Very Constipated."

When we reached Ajanta, we spent a long time climbing up the horseshoe-shaped ravine to visit many of the caves. They are cut into the hillsides; the work started around 200 BC but continued into the sixth and seventh centuries AD. The greatest period was inspired by Buddhism. The paintings are in various stages of decay but, having been done as a kind of fresco using natural pigments, the images and colors were bonded to the walls and quite easy to view in some of the caves. Many of the images are of scenes from the Buddha's life. The general style of the Ajanta paintings would be familiar to anyone who has visited the Indian art section of a major art museum, as all subsequent Indian painting is said to have to have been influenced by Ajanta.

In his interesting, eccentric, anti-British history of India, *The Discovery of India*, Nehru condemns Ajanta for locking Indian art into unchanging forms. This may be true, but we thought Ajanta was magnificent. At least this artistic sterility was one of the few Indian problems that Nehru didn't blame on the British. Whatever caused India's cultural constipation happened centuries before the British arrived.

Nehru also slides over many awkward facts: that the Hindu India he celebrates was ruled and shaped by the Muslim Mughal invaders for centuries before the British landed; that "India" was really no more than a collection of large and small despotic states before the British; and that the idea of one India, an India with a non-mythological, factual history, an India with written records and dates for past events was a British creation. In many ways, the British invented India.

Nehru wrote *The Discovery of India* (in English, of course, since English was his first language) while in a British prison. He was a London-trained British barrister. Nehru never learned to speak any Indian language very well, even though his family were great landowners in Kashmir. Nehru was a Hindu, though the ordinary people in Kashmir are Muslims. Nehru believed fervently in self-determination for India but not for Kashmir, thus creating a festering problem there to this day.

Nehru was a seething mass of contradictions. The British were useful whipping boys for his resulting frustrations. Perhaps that is why Nehru cuckolded Lord Mountbatten, the last Viceroy of India. Or perhaps it was because Lady Mountbatten was bored with the pompous, and allegedly gay, Lord Mountbatten.

From Ajanta we drove to Aurangabad, where we booked ourselves into a massive old hotel, the Station Hotel, which had been built by the Indian railways during the Raj. This hotel exists in a time warp. Even the cutlery in the dining room was Mappin and Webb silver plate. (Mappin and Webb is a fine old London jeweler.)

During dinner, Alyson and I had a fascinating conversation about the ongoing links between the UK and India with an Indian surgeon who had spent years training in Nottingham, England. Alyson is generally much better at striking up conversations with people than I am, but in India I too found this easy.

We went on to Ellora, as important to Indian sculpture as Ajanta is to Indian painting. The setting is a valley with thirty-two caves cut into the rock walls. Done later than Ajanta, the art exhibits Hindu, Buddhist, and Jain elements. Whatever the religious significance, much of the carving is gloriously erotic: men with seven heads having their single massive cock stroked; women with huge breasts pleasuring themselves; gloriously phallic statues of Ganesh, the elephant god. Wandering among the sculptures with us were many cheerful young Indian soldiers who were having a day out in India's past.

<hr>

The next morning, on the way into Bombay, in one swift incident I lost my taste for driving in India. We were making our way down from the hills onto the plain around Bombay. We were already in the shantytown that surrounds the city, when a toddler rushed out across the muddy road in front of Elsie. The small, naked boy was running to his father. I braked so hard that my leg shook afterwards for minutes. The father snatched up the screaming child. People rushed out from the shanties that surrounded the road. The father was relieved, but I realised that we might have been lynched if the child had gone under Elsie.

Then, in the contrasts that India continually offered, we found a charming small hotel, the Fariyas, overlooking a small fishing harbor outside Bombay. Alyson loved this hotel. I was still shaken by nearly killing the child and couldn't talk at dinner. So afterwards we went off to see the first part of the great Russian 1968 version of *War and Peace*. The Indian audience loved the film, especially the wolf hunt with borzois.

On the way back to the hotel, we passed a poor Indian guy lying inertly on the pavement. His eyes were open; his skin had lost color. We thought that he was dead. I hope he was. Everyone walked by him.

The following day we spent with two rascally, but very amusing, Muslim taxi drivers who had persuaded us to go with them in fluent but eccentric English. They showed us various sights for a fee, but mostly we sat in their car, talking.

One driver told a story about three Indian guys who go to New York. One is a Hindu, one is a Muslim, and one is a Sikh. They check into a skyscraper hotel and go out on the town. When they come back to the hotel late at night, they discover that the hotel's elevators are out of action so they will have to walk up seventy-five floors. They agree that each will tell a story on the way up.

First the Hindu and then the Muslim tells his story. They stop at the fiftieth floor. Now it is the Sikh's turn to tell his story, but instead he bursts into tears and, despite their queries, cries all the way up the final twenty-five floors until they reach their room. Once there, the two ask the Sikh why he is crying. "I left the key at the front desk," he replies. The joke was hilarious then because we'd parked to look at the sea and smoked hash for an hour with the two rascals prior to hearing the joke.

They drove us back to the Gateway to India, the massive, arched monument built by the British to impress those arriving in Bombay from the sea. There the drivers dropped us, pointing out some blond hippie beggars behind the Gateway. The drivers said the hippies were Dutch. There was also a young Indian girl holding a dying baby. The hippies were begging for drug money. The girl was begging for food. Leaving us, the two drivers gave money to the Dutch hippies.

From Bombay we flew to Madras. After my near miss with the child, I wasn't going to drive any more than I had to from then on. Flying in India in those days was chaotic but very cheap. Flights were grossly overbooked; airports were primitive and jammed. Security as we now know it was non-existent. Pushing was mandatory. Getting a ticket was only the beginning of the scramble. We enjoyed our flights, despite the fuss. Indians always remained good tempered in such circumstances, and we tried to copy them.

Madras was wonderful; as a boy I had longed to visit it. This was where the British imperial adventure in India began. In 1639, Francis Day of the British East India Company bought a small strip of land on the wonderfully named Coromandel Coast to establish a trading post. Like Bombay, now officially called Mumbai, Madras is now renamed Chennai, but neither Bombay nor Madras had much of an existence before the British. Both were small fishing villages.

Madras grew slowly after the British arrived and was conquered briefly by the French, who were based at Pondicherry just down the coast. However, Madras is today the fourth-largest city of India. Pondicherry is a sleepy enclave where a few older people speak French.

The reason for this disparity is due to one man, Robert Clive, who arrived in Madras in 1744 as a "factor" or "writer" with the East India Company. The role of a writer was neither purely business nor purely military. The young writer sought to make his fortune by whatever means available. Trade was the basic way, but successful trade meant defeating the Company's enemies and rivals. With luck, the writer would make his fortune before the climate or disease killed him. Plump and prematurely aged, the nabob, like Jos Sedley in *Vanity Fair*, would return to England to marry.

When Clive arrived in India, the country was in political turmoil. After the death of the Mughal Emperor Aurangzeb in 1707, the Mughals lost control. Power resided in regional sub-viceroys. The French and the British not only fought against each other directly but sought alliances with various native leaders. Distinguishing himself in skirmishes against the French, Clive was eventually put in charge of the Company's army in Bengal, the area around Calcutta.

On June 22, 1757, Clive led about one thousand European soldiers and two thousand native soldiers, or sepoys, equipped with nine cannons, against some fifty thousand natives and a handful of French. The Battle of Plassey was a total and largely bloodless victory for Clive.

Thus began the process that ended with the inhabitants of a small, wet, distant island ruling a fifth of the human race. So, for anyone who sees adventure or romance in the history of the creation of the British Empire, Madras, by whatever name, is a fascinating place.

From my journal of September 20:

We wandered into St. Andrew's Presbyterian Church early today while an old Indian man was giving organ lessons to a boy. The memorials in the church were touching and very Scottish, such as, To St. John Doe from a few of his more intimate friends.

The high spot of the day was in the afternoon after a huge Anglo-Indian lunch. We took a rickshaw to Fort St. George. The driver was a character who eventually extracted eight rupees from me through charm and hard work. The museum at the Fort was interesting enough, but inside was St. Mary's Church, built in 1680 and of infinitely more interest to me.

In St. Mary's, the parish register contains the entries of the marriages of Robert Clive and of Elihu Yale, whose donation of cloth and books launched Yale University. Elihu Yale never set foot in New Haven; his money went instead. The memorials on the walls to so many young British men who died in their youth moved me, but most moving was the choir of elderly Indian women practicing famous English hymns. Outside the church was a statue of Queen Victoria, garlanded with marigolds, a mark of respect.

We stayed at the aptly named Imperial Hotel. The hotel was excellent, but there were some unpleasant Westerners scattered around Madras. I wrote in a cafe: "Across from me is sitting a drunken American or Canadian who is now, thankfully, unconscious. He is dirty, unshaven, and clutching a stuffed mongoose posed on a stand; the mongoose is chewing a stuffed cobra."

Alyson and I ignored these people, watching in disgust again as poor Indians gave them money. For unrelated reasons, we spent a lot of time in Madras in our room. We'd discovered the fun of sexy wrestling matches. Alyson was sure that she could find some hold that would defeat me. She was wrong, but who was I not to let her try?

For the next few days we immersed ourselves in ancient Tamil India. We went to Kancheepuram, famous for temples to Shiva and for making exquisite saris. Then, on to the sea coast and the Shore Temple at Mahabalipuram. As usual, we had these fascinating places largely to ourselves, though care was needed when walking on the beach to avoid human excrement washed up at the sea's edge.

In India, we were not bothered by beggars much. Perhaps we looked financially unpromising. Instead, we attracted crowds of local men and women who were fascinated by Alyson's tall, blue-eyed English differentness. They had seen Western men, but Alyson was something new.

Some wanted to touch her, which was off-putting but not lewd in intent. Mostly they were happy to look at her as closely as they dared. Alyson's record was seventy-three rural gawkers—men, women and children—when we stopped at a country rail crossing to let a train go by. These amiable folk appeared from nowhere. There are more people everywhere in India than one can possibly anticipate.

From there, we went on by express train to Bangalore. Alyson was sitting next to an elderly, ascetic-looking Tamil man whom we took to be some sort of great religious sage until he pulled out a dog-eared copy of *Women's Own*, a down-market UK magazine for housewives.

We stayed at the Hotel Krishnarajasagar, a grand old British-style hotel that overlooks the wild overflow from the great, long dam on the Kaveri River and the Mughal-style, vast Brindavan Gardens below the dam. Each floor of the hotel had a wide veranda outside the rooms. A manservant sat outside any occupied room. To obtain an ice-cold Kingfisher beer or a pot of excellent tea, all that was necessary was to go to the room's screen door and say, "Beer, please," to the screen. Within moments, the beer would appear. At night the gardens were magical, with illuminated fountains and cleverly placed lights under specimen trees.

We returned to Bangaglore via Srirangapatnam, a fortress island on the Kaveri, once the headquarters of Tippu Sultan, the Muslim ruler of a Hindu state who sided with the French against the British. Tippu fought a series of successful wars in the late 1700s against first-rate British generals like Arthur Wellesley, the future Duke of Wellington. Tippu finally lost and was soon betrayed and murdered by his own people. The British wars in India always had a political dimension that the British excelled at. This was fortunate for the British, because the number of British soldiers available for battle was generally very small.

<hr />

That night we took the overnight train to Cochin. Indian train stations, like Indian airports, appear shambolic but actually work well. With the help of friendly fellow travelers, we found our train and pushed our way onto it. In those days, Indian trains had a number of different classes. Alyson and I were in non-air-conditioned second class. Our compartment was clean, but the ceiling fans were broken, and the berths were just fold-down shelves. The window was half open. Sharing the compartment with us were Mr. Samuel, a Tamil Christian, Naval Officer Sharma, a Hindu from the Punjab, and a very gentle, very quiet Jain, whose name I have lost.

The train, pulled by a steam engine, set off slowly. We assumed that it would speed up, but the train maintained the same slow, steady pace through the night, stopping frequently. At the first long stop, and without our asking, Mr. Samuel hopped off and brought us some chapattis and vegetable curry on a plate of palm leaves. It was delicious. We offered him some of the Indian rum we had but he refused it, observing that a bottle like ours would last him a year. (I was drinking rum from the bottle, as was Alyson.)

Religion is an easy topic of discussion in India. I asked Mr. Samuel how he became a Christian and was put gently in my place. He replied, "My ancestors were converted by St. Thomas the Apostle in the first century." Mr. Samuel then shocked us by explaining that he gave a tenth of his meager income to Oral Roberts, a grasping American radio and TV evangelist. What a vicious long-distance scam to pull on a simple, honest believer.

Naval Officer Sharma had trained at the Royal Navy torpedo school in Wales. He was a lean, handsome, fit-looking man in his thirties. Officer Sharma spoke fluent English and joked that the English language was the best thing the British had brought to India. We talked about Indian politics and the military situation. Officer Sharma did not want war with Pakistan but was certain that war would come, and before Christmas. India would win easily. (Both these forecasts were spot on.)

Though a Hindu, Officer Sharma was reading a paperback edition of the Old Testament Book of Daniel. He was a most interesting man. I have often wished that I had his address.

While we were talking, the Jain listened and nodded but said nothing. We folded down the bunks, but sleep did not come easily, and we talked off and on through the night. The chuff-chuff of the steam engine was soothing and reminded me of visiting my grandmother in Glendale, Ohio, as a small child and listening to the same sounds from the Baltimore and Ohio engines as they pulled out of the Glendale station.

Smuts from the steam engine poured in through the window. We stopped frequently at brightly lighted stations, full of noisy, shouting people even in the middle of the night. Neither of us slept much, but we lay quietly listening to the clickety-clack of the train's wheels. The Jain and Mr. Samuel rose briskly at 6:00 a.m.; Officer Sharma had gotten off while we slept. Alyson and I looked at each other in a shattered sort of way; the train came into Cochin and we hopped off.

We loved every minute of this train journey and still talk about it, forty years on.

———◆———

Cochin was mostly about rain. We visited the oldest synagogue in India and St. Francis' Church where Vasco da Gama's body was parked for some years. We peered through the rain at the famous Chinese fishing nets and ate in a Chinese restaurant. Then we gave up on Cochin and went on to Goa, where it was also pouring.

Very sodden, we arrived back in Bombay and picked up Elsie. Despite my determination not to drive any more, we set off by road for Rajasthan in good spirits. Predictably, the drive turned out to be horrendous. A Tata truck creamed past us on the passenger side, smashed off the wing mirror, and showered Alyson with glass, cutting her hand. I was furious. I hopped out, grabbed a rock, and went belting down the road after the truck. Lookers-on shouted at me in the local language, and I shouted back in English in a highly neo-colonialist way. Of course, the truck was gone in a cloud of dust.

Cooling down (and reproached firmly by Alyson), I hoped that the incomprehension between me and the lookers-on was mutual. Some hours later, a small boy threw a large rock at us. He missed. Tough day.

We stayed that night, October 1, at the Government Rest House at Navsari, many long hours from Bombay. The rest house was tidier than the Dak bungalow and insect free, but I noted that the "sheets are too foul to call it clean." Alyson also refused to use the water bucket for a shower, very unlike her, but the water was smelly and somehow icy cold.

That night I tried to analyze why I let traffic incidents make me so angry. Partially it was the heat; partially the sheer fecklessness of so many of the people, kind and gentle though they always were face to face. But the same man who literally would not step on an ant might casually kill ten people by truly lunatic driving, or let his child be disfigured by smallpox even though there was a free government inoculation clinic in the nearest town. India was a country of paradoxes.

The next day was no easier, despite a wonderful start. We rose early and were having a coffee with buffalo milk, bananas, and chapattis in the cool of the morning when we heard the schoolgirls at the school next to the government rest house singing the Indian national anthem. We had heard snatches of it before but never sung properly.

Called the *Jana Gana Mana*, the Bengali words are a hymn to the God of All Gods by the poet and Nobel Prize winner, Tagore. The tune is thrilling. We got up from the breakfast table and listened to the young girls, in their uniforms of white blouses and dark blue skirts, sing loudly with feeling. Each verse ends with a rising cry of *Jaya, Jaya, Jaya, Jaya, he*! Or "Victory, Victory, Victory Victory to Thee!"

Fired up, we hit the road at 8:00 a.m. We made brisk progress through Baroda (now called Vadodara) and thought we would cruise our way to Rajasthan. But I had not reckoned on the challenges offered by Ahmadabad.

This industrial megalopolis was the center of the Indian textile industry and known as the Manchester of the East. (Incidentally, it is a total myth that the British didn't allow a textile industry to develop in India.) Ahmadabad is a Gujarati city, and Gujaratis, often named Patel, have been good at business since the dawn of time. Industry came naturally to them. Under the British there were large, active stock exchanges in India and a well-developed banking system, so capital could be mobilized.

Ahmadabad had grown in a sprawling, uncontrolled way into a city of millions and by 1971 had the traffic and smog problems of LA on a bad, bad day. However, even in October it was hotter and more humid than LA could ever be. And we needed to drive right through it from south to north. We spent three hours lost in Ahmadabad. We asked policemen on foot to point us to the way out of the city. They patiently and politely led us into dead end streets, solid with traffic. We asked pedestrians to direct us. Alas, the pedestrians proved not to know exactly where they were, let alone how to direct someone in a car.

I showed people maps. Alyson showed people maps. Considering that no one appeared to have ever seen a map before, they paid close attention as we pointed at locations on the map. Everyone was helpful and kind. And useless. Some people misdirected us, especially if we gave the slightest sign of wanting to go in a certain direction. "That is the right and only direction," they would say, shaking their heads in our "no" that means "yes" in India. I remained more or less calm. Eventually a motorcycle cop took pity on us. We followed him out of the city onto the road north to Rajasthan.

Gandhi began his campaign of civil disobedience to the British in Ahmadabad. We may have been belated Western recipients of this great tradition. Or, as Alyson wryly observed in her diary, 'To enjoy Indian travel away from tourist places requires the saintly patience of the Mahatma. In addition to having the immune system of a mongoose."

In an epitaph, Kipling anticipated our problem: "A Fool lies here who tried to hustle the East."

Later—much, much later—we reached Udaipur in Rajasthan and tried to stay at the famous Lake Palace Hotel. We arrived in moonlight, full of romantic thoughts. The moon was reflected in the lovely, millpond-still lake. There were sweet night fragrances. The Lake Palace Hotel floated serenely in the middle of the lake as it does in the famous tourist ad.

But the Lake Palace was full or didn't want guests that looked as shattered and dirty as we did. Feeling a bit depressed, we stayed in a dull, yet perfectly good, hotel on the shore of the lake. That night Alyson began to show the symptoms of the tropical virus that was to bother her for years afterwards. She was feverish, difficult, and miserable. "A surpassingly horrid day," I recorded at bedtime.

The driving continued to be challenging. In Rajasthan we encountered large numbers of ill or malnourished men on high, sit-up bicycles, copies of the black British Raleigh bikes of my childhood. These poor guys wobbled from one side of the road to the other in unpredictable, lurching movements, so Alyson called them "Rajasthani wobblers." Their death wish was pronounced. Once we saw a blind adult bicyclist being vocally guided by a child riding a smaller bike behind the adult. Alyson called this "wobbling back to Jesus."

We paused in Jaipur, the dry, pink-stone capital of Rajasthan, to look at the beautiful miniature paintings there. There were tiny exquisite scenes of Rajput princes pig sticking, of bull elephants fighting, and of beautiful women in court.

Back in Delhi, we spent several days recharging our batteries and our finances. Alyson was appalled by her first experience of financial black markets, just as she was when I sold my underwear. The money-changing technique was simple enough. We would walk down one of the main streets feeding into the Connaught Circle. Out of nowhere would appear seedy-looking guys who would offer to change money. I would ask the rate against the dollar or the Swiss franc or the Deutschmark—I had some of each—and, after listening to one or two of these seedy rascals, I would go off into a nearby building with the chosen scoundrel. Inside a filthy, hot office, the guy would sit down behind a desk like a real businessman.

I would push across a $50 bill. It would be closely examined. A metal box would be pulled out from under the desk. A wad of dirty, ragged Indian rupees was casually taken from the box. Notes were stripped from the wad with much licking of fingers. I was then handed the rupees, which I would ostentatiously count. Alyson would be waiting for me back on the street, grim faced.

I am afraid that I let her think that this was a dangerous activity. I actually thought that there was no danger at all in changing money in broad daylight. Why would some money changer attack me and risk being arrested for currency offenses? Plus, my impression was that the Indian authorities tolerated the handful of tourists who used the black market since the official rate of exchange was ludicrous. Officially, the rate was around 7.50 rupees for $1. Realistically, the rate was 20-30 rupees for $1.

Nepal

After a few days in Delhi, we flew to Nepal despite both of us feeling increasingly ill. This flight was a peculiar experience that induced in me the same intense fear I remembered from flying in and out of isolated fire bases in Vietnam.

On the morning of the flight, and with some difficulty, we found the Air Nepal counter in the chaotic outer reaches of the Delhi airport, having battled our way through hoards of humanity just to get into the terminal building. The approach to the counter was blocked by a seething crowd that seemed less patient than usual. However, I chalked this up to there only being one ticket clerk behind the counter. We had plenty of time before the flight; our tickets appeared to be kosher, so we stood calmly at the back of the crowd.

An hour passed, and I began to fear that we would miss the flight. I elbowed my way to the front of the crowd to find out what was going on. The ticket guy gave me a sad smile. "The plane is delayed," he said, "but not to worry. They are working on the problem."

"What problem?" I asked.

"Oh, sir, the pilot is being drunk."

"Drunk! For heaven's sake, get another pilot!"

"There is only one pilot available today, but they are giving him many cups of coffee. Everything will be A-OK."

We were about to fly in the direction of Mount Everest in a twin-engine Fokker flown by a semi-sober pilot who would need to pee every fifteen minutes. Wonderful.

When, hours later, the flight was announced, Alyson and I looked at each other. We flew. We both had such awful headaches from our illnesses that the flight would be a distraction. And it was. The views were spectacular, especially during the brief periods that the Fokker wasn't being thrown up and down by air currents. The landing at Katmandu was like driving Elsie with broken shock absorbers. There were no announcements. Someone opened the plane doors; we poured ourselves out and headed for a cheap hotel.

That evening, despite our fevers, we went to the splendid Soaltee Hotel, where Alyson had a letter of introduction to the owner. This was a great success since the owner was a Rana, a member of the family that ruled Nepal for centuries as hereditary prime ministers. We were invited to a grand party that evening for Australian travel agents and lavishly wined and dined. Unfortunately, we felt so lousy that we didn't stay long.

The next morning, October 9, I left Alyson in bed and wandered around Katmandu. In those days it was still a quaint and peculiar city of temples and old wooden buildings and streets full of numerous sacred cows. Quite apart from the output of the cows, the streets were filthy, potholed, and without drains.

A leper was begging outside the US Information Agency library when I went in to read about Nepal. No one gave him money because no one went near him. In Kathmandu no urging was needed to make you wash your hands frequently.

Katmandu Street 1971

We stayed in a simple hotel, the Manashu, and Alyson couldn't sleep because of mosquitoes. Nevertheless, she insisted on getting up the next day, and we bicycled to Bodhnath about ten kilometers from Katmandu. Approaching Bodhnath, we saw from quite a distance the massive Buddhist stupa that towers above the town. The stupa is a mound-like building in the shape of a half-sphere that is used as a Buddhist reliquary.

For centuries, Bodhnath was a stop on the trading route of Tibetan Buddhists; now it was the site of Tibetan refugee camps. We wandered through the market stalls of the refugees. In one we were smitten by a droll little grey Shih Tzu dog, whom we instantly coveted. I think that Alyson liked him in part because he tried to bite me. The woman and her husband somehow communicated to us how they had fled Tibet and come over the 14,000 foot passes in 1959 with only their religion, their children, and their dogs. (Before we had children, we acquired our first Shih Tzu. I buried the last, Tinso, in our garden in Connecticut in 2008.) Some Tibetan children started singing, and Alyson impulsively kissed me. The husband said, "They singing so sweet."

Bicycling back to Katmandu, we both felt better. We decided to go and have a closer look at Mt. Everest the next day.

To view Mt. Everest, we were told it was necessary to take a bus from Katmandu to Daman. If the clouds lifted, the mighty mountain could be seen clearly from there. Daman was a mere local bus ride from Katmandu.

Accordingly, we turned up at the bus station at 6:00 a.m. The driver was a cheerful, mad Sikh who put Alyson on one of the front seats by the window. I fought my way to the back of the bus. Three hours of curve after curve, looking down sick-making drop offs, and bone-jarring thumping followed before we arrived at the long, high ridge where Daman sits at nine thousand feet.

We lugged our stuff up to the Everest Point Motel, which consisted of a round, concrete tower with an observation room at the top and a small wooden shed next to the tower where we were to sleep. We went to sit in the observation room, which doubled as a restaurant. It was cool and cloudy outside, and there was no view of Everest. But the valley below the tower was beautiful and terraced for farming from just below the tower to the bottom of the valley, thousands of feet below. Around the tower were large wild rhododendrons.

We were given tea and asked what we wanted for dinner. However, the young boy who waited on us soon made it clear that the only correct answer was chicken with rice. Fine, we said, bring on the chicken with rice. A few minutes later, we saw the young boy, armed with a long bamboo pole, chasing a splendid green-and-red jungle fowl cock down the hillside. Bam! He knocked it down and brought it back to the tower, holding it by the feet. The rice came from the terraces, we assumed. Eat local. It was very good.

We decided to go to sleep early and hope to see Everest at dawn. We brought the double sleeping bag. We got into it, pulled up the zipper, and I was just about to put out the candle when Alyson said, "Don't look up."

Quickly looking up at the low ceiling, I saw the thing of my worst nightmares—an enormous spider, the biggest spider I have ever seen. Orange-brown and hairy, with a body the size of an avocado stone, it was a good eight inches across. I panicked totally.

Ejecting myself from the zipped-up sleeping bag, I cursed Alyson royally for slowing me down. Before she had a chance to resent this, the spider scurried at unbelievable speed down the wall in our direction. Alyson bravely slapped at it with her sandal, missed, then screamed in fear and rage as it rushed across the floor at her. By this time, I was past the shaking-and-gibbering-with-fear stage and somehow managed to grab the water bucket and throw most of the contents on the spider. This made it ball up. I crushed it with the doormat. Yes, I know that large spiders are harmless to humans. You had to be there.

Mount Everest was still invisible at dawn and through the morning, so we abandoned our hope of seeing it. But we enjoyed ourselves thoroughly, wandering around and chatting with some cute kids. One little boy gave Alyson an orchid that had the most subtle and delicious scent. I wasn't even too annoyed when a snotty, middle-aged American couple refused to let us share their mini bus back to Katmandu. We waited for the afternoon local bus instead.

The bus driver was the same cheerful and totally mad Sikh. I went to the back of the bus as before. This time I sat next to a young Nepalese man whose baby daughter was in the arms of his ill-looking wife across from us. His small son was next to the wife. After the bus started down the ridge and hit the first switchback, I understood why the man didn't sit with his family. Immediately after the first swerving curve, the man was violently sick all over himself. The smell was atrocious. I opened the bus window beside him and managed to help him lean part way out so he could barf down the side of the bus.

The dirt road went through numerous narrow, one-tight-lane bridges. Every time I saw a bridge coming up, I pulled his limp form back into the bus. He was pathetically grateful. In truth, I didn't want to sit next to someone without a head. The children moved over to sympathize with their daddy. I held the little boy so that he wouldn't be thrown around.

When we returned to Delhi, we were both so ill that we checked back into the Jan Path Hotel, though we were running low on money. Alyson went to bed. I didn't feel like going very far from a loo, so I stayed around the hotel. From our room we watched a major Hindu wedding procession. The bejeweled groom was mounted on an immaculate white horse, preceded by a large band skillfully playing the "Colonel Bogey March." The Raj lives on.

That evening I was wandering in the gloomy hotel corridors when I met a large, jolly Sikh of about thirty-five. We chatted for a while, and then he suggested that I return to his room and join his friends for a party. This soon turned into an absolutely wild affair with much drink and raucous music from a boogie box. I liked every Sikh that we met. They are crazy drivers, but they have a strong sense of carpe diem.

We both celebrated my birthday, October 20, by feeling better. Alyson gave me a wonderful old brass statue of Kali and a tiny stone one of Ganesh. Both statues still look at me daily. But, feeling better or not, we made a painful decision. We had planned to stay in India through the winter and go to Kashmir. However, my money was running out, and worse, India and Pakistan were about to go to war. Everyone knew this. We might be stuck penniless in India indefinitely. Plus the Indians might seize Elsie the VW for the war effort, leaving me with the obligation to pay back the UK bank for the carnet, or customs guarantee.

Also, if we left too late and the passes in eastern Turkey were closed by snow, we would be stuck for the winter in Iran, an even more unattractive prospect. The passes were open most years until late December, so we had plenty of time if we hustled.

We drove up into the Punjab from Delhi, the start of our long drive back to London. We spent the night in Chandigarh, a new city designed by Le Corbusier towards the end of his career. Chandigarh stands apart from any other city in Asia and must constantly surprise the Punjabis who wander through its streets. We speculated on who was the more crazy; Le Corbusier for plunking down one of his brutal European concrete visions in the middle of the Punjab, or the Punjabi politicians who approved this peculiar and inappropriate expenditure.

By getting up at dawn in Chandigarh, we reached the Indo-Pakistan border in time to cross it the same day. Not having had my experiences crossing Asian land borders, Alyson couldn't understand why I was jumpy. I was grateful for her soothing presence, but there were a number of matters to worry about. There was the small matter of the large hole in the dash where the Blaupunkt radio I'd sold had been. I put some maps and papers in the hole.

But how to account for all the other things that I had sold? And how to present the Indian customs guy with the bogus statement of all the money that I had with me? Casually? Calmly but assertively? I had made this statement more or less jibe with the amount of money I'd declared coming into India, less months of expenses, but neither statement was close to reality. I also had some undeclared, large-denomination dollar bills inside my socks. Would they make me strip?

If questioned, I intended to thrust a massive wad of receipts, hotel bills, and the like into the hands of the customs officer and hope that he would be too busy to bother with them. I also had a twenty-dollar bill handy to slip to the customs guy inside my passport, but that was a desperation move.

My real hope was that the sheer novelty of Alyson would dazzle the customs guy as much as she had dazzled Indians wherever we went. And lo, such proved to be the case. We were waved through with a smile by a friendly Indian officer. I told Alyson that she was the most wonderful thing that had ever happened to me.

We drove across no man's land on a raised causeway between two heavily mined swamps. When we reached the Pakistani crossing point, I braced myself for trouble. The swarthy, tough soldiers there looked inclined to be difficult, which meant many, many hours of waiting and much groveling and supplicating.

These sub-machine-gun carrying military customs officers were about to order us to unload the vehicle when they spotted that day's Indian newspaper on the back seat.

"Can we have it?" they asked.

"But of course," I said.

Pakistan had just thrashed India at field hockey, which was then the national sport and obsession of both countries. This defeat was headlined in big type. The Indian field hockey captain's weeping, turbaned, and heavily mustached photo covered the front page. The Pakistani officials wanted to gloat while reading about India's sporting collapse in an Indian newspaper. Distracted, they waved us through.

The date we crossed the border was October 24, 1971. On December 3, 1971, the long-awaited Indo-Pakistan war exploded. A column of Pakistani tanks surged across that causeway, only to be obliterated by Indian firepower. At sea, Indian Navy Officer Sharma and his shipmates sank most of the Pakistani navy in a few days. Both sides fought bravely, but Pakistan was completely outgunned. The war ended on December 16 with the total defeat of Pakistan and the succession and transformation of East Pakistan into Bangladesh.

Back to Afghanistan

After a night in Rawalpindi, we left Pakistan by driving up the Khyber Pass. Alyson noted that we followed the Khyber River higher and higher, with the river becoming narrower and narrower until it was just a dribble between large boulders. Numerous nomads with their sheep and camels climbed up on foot. Sections of the road's pavement were missing or broken into large chunks, rocking Elsie despite her expensive new shock absorbers. The passing traffic blew hot, plentiful dust in through our open windows, richly seasoned with finely ground sheep and camel droppings.

It was good to be back in Kabul, not a place you expect to visit more than once in a lifetime. But we weren't fit enough for an expansive Kabul experience. Alyson was ill again with apparent strep throat. I was again enjoying some virulent form of diarrhea or even dysentery. India has germs that simply overwhelm the immune systems of even the healthiest young western adults. Now the germs were merrily traveling along with us.

We checked into the Mustafa Hotel, which claimed to offer all modern comforts. The hotel was indeed in a new building but already had achieved "a sleazy charm" according to my journal. The Mustafa had only intermittent running water that was either boiling hot or freezing cold, regardless of which tap you tried. The toilet was flushed with a bucket, but at least it wasn't another "Persian version." Theoretically, there was some form of heating. Nights were cold, starry, and very dry.

By the morning of October 26, I was seriously worried about Alyson. Looking down her throat, I could see nothing but raw flesh. Plus she had a high fever. Being a traditional English stoic and public school girl, she did not complain, but I knew that we urgently had to do something.

First, we made our way to the local Afghan hospital. This was in a relatively new Russian-style building, but everything else about the hospital was straight out of a medieval plague hospital. While we were waiting, a young Afghan man was carried in on a wooden door used as a stretcher. He was about twenty and had been mauled by an animal, according to gestures made by the men carrying him. Possibly by a bear. The young man stared up at the ceiling with big, dark-brown eyes. He made no sound and showed no signs of pain, though his chest was ripped open. His bloody, shredded clothes were flung over him. His face had the pallor of death. There were flies everywhere. Their buzzing was in stark contrast to the silence of the people in the room.

We got up and left, feeling out of place in that room of grim, wordless suffering. We wandered around the streets of Kabul, stunned. And, through sheer luck, we ran into Richard, an English doctor about my age, and Richard's wife, also a doctor. This kind couple had been on their way overland by bus to India to help in some clinic. On reaching Kabul, they had discovered that many in the hippie community were ill with everything from intestinal parasites to venereal diseases. Hepatitis from various shared vices was particularly common. Richard and his wife, whose name I have sadly lost, considered themselves to be first-century Christians. They decided that the hippies were lost souls in need, so they lingered in Kabul.

Richard came back to the Mustapha Hotel with us, had Alyson sit down on the metal-framed cot and peered down her throat. Without a lab, Richard said that he couldn't be absolutely certain that she had strep throat, but she should start on an antibiotic at once. And he thought that a sulfa drug would put my guts right. I expected him then to write prescriptions. These, he said, were completely unnecessary. In Kabul, every sort of European and American drug from powerful antibiotics to opiates could be bought over the counter in one of the large general stores on Pushtunistan Square. Richard wrote the names of the drugs we needed on a scrap of paper. He would not accept anything in return. Not a thing.

I rushed out to buy the drugs. Just as Richard had said, every sort of drug was available. I showed the Afghan sales clerk Richard's list, after adding a large quantity of Valium to it. (You never know when a Valium might come in handy.) The next day we felt no better but dragged ourselves off to the Iranian consulate to obtain Iranian visas. Once again, anything connected with Iran was unlucky for me. Upon arriving, I found that Elsie had a flat tire. Then we found that there was quite a waiting line since the Iranian functionary at the door would only let two people into the building at a time.

When we were ushered in to see the smug, unpleasant Iranian consul, he first shook us down for ten dollars before deigning to accept the normal small visa fees and our photos. We would have our visas two days later, he said. "Oh, and you, but not the woman, will need a cholera inoculation to enter Iran." Apparently, Brits did not bring cholera into Iran and did not need a cholera inoculation but Americans, well-known as cholera carriers, were required to have this inoculation.

So, after changing the tire, we went across the Kabul River to the blocks of neo-Stalinist flats built by the Russians. There we found with some difficulty the inoculation section of the Afghan Ministry of Public Health. This was a very small and very dirty room, probably reflecting the importance of public health in the Afghan scheme of things. A male medical type agreed to inject me, and I rolled up my sleeve in anticipation.

Then, unfortunately, there was some ugly shouting by me. The turbaned medical guy was going to use the same needle that I had just seen him use on the previous patient. The guy showed by gesticulation that the needle was still nice and sharp. No blunt needles for this experienced practitioner. He grabbed my arm forcefully. Luckily, a helpful Afghan man, who was also waiting for some injection, intervened before the medic's blood was drawn by me. A new Russian needle was taken out of what I hoped was a sterile package, and I submitted.

On the way back into the center of Kabul, an Afghan in a white VW Beetle swerved into us. Or so it seemed to me. Alyson considered that the accident was due to my taking a Valium the night before. There was more ugly shouting until Alyson persuaded the other driver and me to go to the excellent VW garage where one of the two fat, friendly owners convinced the VW-driving Afghan to accept two hundred afghani in settlement.

We spent the afternoon resting back at the Mustafa Hotel. Alyson wrote in her diary that the "lovely smell of hashish was a pleasing contrast with the blocked-drain smells all over the hotel." She added that "adversity is good for us." The penicillin had begun to work its magic, and Alyson noted "thank you, Alexander Fleming."

While we felt so lousy, we read each other snatches of Eric Newby's *A Short Walk in the Hindu Kush*. Raved about by Evelyn Waugh, this traveler's tale is the funniest and best evocation of the wildness and wonder of lost Afghanistan that I know, as it is of a now-extinct type of English traveler.

The book contains a remarkable description of travelling in Nuristan, the wildest part of Afghanistan. The Nuristanis remained pagan idol worshipers until the nineteenth century, when they were forcibly converted to Islam. Their culture is distinctive in a country of distinctive cultures. The book offers snippets from a short phrasebook of the Nuristani language. The translated phrases give a sense of the qualities of these remarkably difficult and dangerous tribesmen.

Here are some examples:

Ia chitt bitto tu jarlom.
"I have an intention to kill you."

Or, for a real conversation starter:

Zhi mare badist taw o ayo kakkok daifi gwa.
"A lammergeyer came down from the sky and took off my cock."

Don't go to Afghanistan without reading this small masterpiece. It has never been out of print.

On Friday, October 29, we felt well enough to go for a long walk all around Kabul. In those days, much of the modern, new downtown was done in a vaguely neo-Stalinist style of architecture. The buildings were recent, built in the 1960s and early 1970s. The Russian atmosphere was reinforced by the Soviet helmets on the Afghan soldiers and their goose-stepping in the Russian manner.

In the brilliant autumn sunshine, Kabul looked splendid. There were palaces and gardens and tree-lined avenues, even traffic policemen in white uniforms and white gloves.

Few of the buildings we saw while walking around Kabul that sunny day survived the wars that began so shortly after we left.

The recent destruction of Kabul is only the latest in a long series. In 1929, for example, four kings sat—three only briefly—on the throne in Kabul. The fourth, Nadir Shah, sacked Kabul as part of his victory celebration. Attending his accession the following year was difficult because only one hotel with four rooms was left standing in Kabul.

Nadir Shah defeated the British in the Third Anglo-Afghan War of 1919. This did not, however, prevent him from using British support to gain the throne in 1929. Nadir, a traditionalist, eliminated his predecessor with the Afghan trifecta: stoning, shooting, and hanging. Nadir himself lasted until 1933 before he was assassinated.

No one with the vaguest knowledge of Afghan history can be oblivious to the possibility of sudden and violent political activity in Kabul. Political hazards, of course, are quite apart from the everyday dangers of Afghan life for tourists and locals alike. The day Alyson and I arrived in Kabul, a Swiss girl had been shot, and later died, for the offense of wearing a miniskirt in the wrong part of Kabul.

That afternoon, we were briefly caught up in a demonstration that I described in my journal as mullahs vs. modernists—bearded, turbaned men displaying the green banners of Islam against the red swatches of their clean-shaven, bareheaded Communist opponents. There was pushing and violent shouting. Beards and guns go together in Afghanistan. There were a lot of beards on view.

In those days, apart from those Communists who were academics, only the business-suited officials walking between the government buildings in Kabul were clean shaven and generally unarmed. None of this crowd was in business suits, and not all Communists were unarmed academics. We scuttled.

The next day, I assumed, was the last we would ever spend in Kabul. To celebrate we went to the Khyber Restaurant. We drank a great deal of what was labeled as Afghan wine. After a good deal of giggling about this and that, Alyson refused to tell me something that she had muttered under her breath.

I said that I would scream if she did not tell me. She did not. I gave a long, sustained walrus bellow, causing our fellow diners to jump. After that it seemed tactful to leave, returning to our room to smoke hashish. And, I hoped, to do other things. However, totally without warning, Alyson was very, very sick many, many times. Was it bad wine? Or Allah's way of punishing a drunken kafir (unbeliever) for drinking local wine?

On October 31, we set out early on the road back to Iran, taking the same southerly route across the high, arid semi-desert via Kandahar and Herat. With us we had Dave and Jacqui, two Brits who were simply appalling.

Agreeing with Dave and Jacqui that they could come with us had completely skipped my mind. The sight of them at 6:00 a.m. was a shock. They had lots of zits, lots of hair, and lots of prominent bad teeth. And they smelled a bit. Well, more than a bit. But, to be honest, probably I did too. Apart from Alyson, everyone on the road was a little niffy. Dave and Jacqui shared the driving costs cheerfully enough. Also, some aspect of Alyson's cool reaction to them must have hit home; they were quiet. Or maybe they simply felt as lousy as we did.

Cruising along what was in 1971 a pretty good, well-paved road, we did not stop in Kandahar and drove for twelve hours on the flat, empty road until it was almost dark. Elsie was nearly out of gas, so we finally stopped at a squat, cinder-block roadside building that called itself the Hotel Russia. A gas station was just up the road from it. A few shacks formed the rest of the town. The place looked beyond awful, but we were too tired to go on.

Alyson had been fantasizing about a hot meal, but the grim-featured desk clerk took pleasure in explaining to us in sign language that this dump had no electricity, no running water, and no food. Exhausted, we took two rooms without the usual haggling about the price. Alyson boiled up a dehydrated meal for all of us on the Camping Gaz stove in our room. The night that followed was quite something. There was no bedding. We huddled on bare mattresses in the cold, remarking to each other from time to time that we had not realized that insects could remain so bitingly active in so cold a room.

In the morning, Alyson said that she would settle the bill. I came downstairs to find her locked in an argument with the repulsive Afghan desk clerk. Though they did not share two words of any language, the point of the argument was clear. Despite our awful night, the desk clerk, whose intense bad breath formed an invisible cloud around his head, was overcharging us, based upon some utterly hypothetical extras. It was simple extortion.

Dave and Jacqui were already sitting in Elsie in front of the hotel. I stood mutely by Alyson, unsure what to do, until she coolly informed the clerk that we were not going to pay one afghani and stormed out, followed by me, but not too quickly for me to notice the man's nasty little eyes go to pinpricks of rage. His screams followed us as we drove away.

Alas, I had forgotten Elsie's need for gas, and this let us down badly. The only gas station was a few hundred yards up the road. We filled up at the single pump, paid, and started to pull out, when several shabby, blank-faced Afghan soldiers armed with AK-47s lowered a bar across the gas station's exit. We could see the long, two-lane road to freedom just beyond the bar. In a film, I would have driven through the flimsy bar. Given Elsie's sloth-like acceleration, that wasn't a practical idea. We had to go back to the Hotel Russia and pay, while absorbing another dose of the clerk's foul breath.

Once we calmed down, driving through the wild Afghan countryside offered familiar pleasures. The land from Kandahar to Herat is barren, but there are views to the north of brown hills with mountains behind. To the south there are irrigated areas. Plus there are the usual mud forts and ruined caravanserais. Every once in a while we would stop at a chai cafe. There, among truck drivers and shepherds, we would sit on cushions or low benches around the samovar, drinking strong black tea in unlimited amounts for a few pennies a head. The other tea drinkers were incurious and formally courteous.

Shepherd with Bike and Dog

Reaching Herat, Alyson was thrilled by the wonderful minarets, even though the first hotel we tried promised us a room, and then cancelled the reservation when we returned. Alyson loved the Herat bazaar, the hot sun, and the clear, cold air. We watched a rug weaver who was watched also by his large white dog, a tame white pigeon, and a thrush singing in a cage. We followed a small boy who was leading a pet lamb with his arm around the lamb's neck.

Alyson tried on embroidered Afghan sheepskin coats but was put off by the strong, lingering aroma of the original wearer. She did, though, buy a lapis ring from a friendly guy in the bazaar. Finally, we went to the great Friday Mosque where Alyson marveled at the thousand-year-old turquoise, blue, and yellow tiles. Outside the mosque, we listened to the muezzin proclaim, with just his huge voice and no speakers, that there is no God but God and Muhammad is his Prophet.

Then we checked into the Bezhad Hotel. This was not a high spot. Apart from the normal lack of plumbing and hot water, the only heating was a wood stove in our room. As soon as the sun went down, it was freezing. I had to buy wood for the stove in small bundles. (I would cheerfully have burnt a chair, but there was none.)

That evening I had reason for the second time to curse Alyson's homeopathic quack doctor in London, Dr. Chandra Sharma, MD (failed) Bombay. And I had reason to be glad that we had the wood stove.

Alyson was repacking her kit after managing to wash some of her underthings. Through some miracle or just snoopiness, I glanced at what she was doing. Lying open on top of the clothes she was packing was a cloth bag full of what appeared to be small, single-use syringes. Dozens of them. Each syringe was full of an opaque, inky substance.

"What are those?" I asked, as calmly as I could.

"Oh, nothing," said Alyson.

"No, they are not nothing; they are syringes. Things for injecting yourself with. Things with needles. And they are full of something."

"Oh, those little things. They are full of vitamin B and squids' ink. Dr. Sharma gave them to me for depression."

"But," said I, "you aren't depressed."

"Dr. Sharma thought that I might be."

It transpired that Dr. Sharma sent Alyson to India without being inoculated for smallpox, polio, tetanus, or typhoid but had at least considered her emotional well-being.

Dr. Sharma, however, had not considered the emotional wellbeing of a young man about to drive a cargo of apparent drug paraphernalia into a country where suspected drug dealers were summarily executed by a prompt hanging. And I wouldn't even be a suspected drug dealer; solid evidence in the form of dozens of neat little syringes would hand some mad dog prosecutor an unimpeachable case.

We then had a major row. Alyson was sure that any Iranian customs official would send a squids' ink syringe off to be tested at the national crime lab. I was even surer that any Iranian police official would simply lock me up, ring up the traveling judge to order the necessary paperwork, and wait to enjoy seeing a ferangi enjoy traditional Iranian justice about two mornings later.

"Besides," said a tearful Alyson, "this argument is making me depressed. I may need a squids' ink injection at any moment."

Fortunately, the wood stove was already burning well. After many tears, Alyson finally accepted that watching the hanging of someone she regularly slept with might be more depressing than not having a squids' ink fix. I put the bag and syringes in the fire. I wasn't worried about someone finding the needles in the stove's ashes. Not in Afghanistan in those druggy days.

More Iranian Bullshit

The next day, November 2, we left Afghanistan. I felt pangs about leaving this wonderful place but even greater pangs in my lower regions, which Alyson cheerfully alluded to as "Tony had a disaster on the way—bare-bottomed agony in the desert."

Worse was to come. The Iranian customs guys had found 250 pounds of hashish in an English car the day before. So they searched everything in Elsie and everything on us. Twice. And slowly.

When I tried to say something helpful about how to get out the spare tire, an Iranian in a karakul cap screamed, "I working here; you no tell me." I shut up, despite the pangs. A full-body cavity search was an unbearable thought.

Driving on to Mashhad, we visited the great shrine, this time without problems, then went carpet shopping. While we were sitting around later in the lobby of a luxury hotel having drinks with Ulf and Hans, a couple of Germans we'd met, Alyson was picked up by an Iranian called Fred, an anglicized version of Firouz. Fred was a large, fleshy guy who was educated, he said, in the UK and the US and certainly spoke fluent American English. We both found Fred charming and amusing, though I wondered exactly what he hoped for from Alyson. Spontaneously, Fred invited us to stay with him in Tehran. When he even drew us a complicated map of how to find him, I felt badly about my suspicions and thanked him profusely.

Tehran is at the foot of the Elburz Mountains, which separate it from the Caspian Sea. In 1971, Tehran was a boom town. Oil and the Shah's encouragement of a secular middle class had turned the city into a sort of LA, complete with broad avenues, smog, and traffic problems. In my opinion, it is no coincidence that Iranians who immigrate to the US home in on southern California.

Oil wealth had unleashed a flash flood of the largest and most expensive Mercedes and BMW cars into the normal Middle Eastern mix of particle-spewing diesel trucks, motorbikes, and buses. The drivers of the Mercedes and BMWs had gone from having no money and no influence to having both within a short period but without gaining any sense of responsibility or acquiring any driving skills along the way. What, after all, was the point of having a Mercedes 500 if you couldn't blast your way through the traffic with your horn while going 150 kilometers per hour?

We found Fred at his tennis club, The Taj, as arranged. Fred was playing an intense game of backgammon. He said over his shoulder to us that we were to return to the club later. In the meantime, we went to the Hilton hotel high above the city to change some money and to use the clean hotel loos for a wash-up.

On the way there, Alyson and I were shaken by the sight of a gruesome accident. Alyson wrote: "I saw my first really bad accident. A half torso at a nightmarish angle through the windows. Blood and limbs strewn over the road." Over the next few days, we would see a number of these tableaus. There appeared to be no urgency to tidy them up. None of the local drivers paid the least attention to them. I saw more fresh dead in Tehran than I'd seen as a soldier in Vietnam.

Back at the Taj Club, Fred was still engrossed in backgammon and distinctly displeased to see us. We sat in the sun watching him until a friendly Turkish businessman, called Alex, asked us to join him for lunch. Alex, who had made a quick fortune importing European toilets into Iran, told us wild and funny tales about his visits to the world's great nightclubs, until Fred grudgingly let us follow him home in his massive BMW. On the way, Fred picked up his downcast, faded-blonde German wife and his silent, sickly daughter of six who was covered with cold sores.

Fred lived in a pseudo-Hollywood mansion that had every luxury but was freezing. No food was offered to us, which is a clear insult in the Middle East. Openly unpleasant by now, Fred wanted us to sleep in separate rooms, but Alyson and I crammed into a small room at the back of the house with one bed, no sheets, and a single blanket.

I brought in a heavy wrench, which I placed beside the narrow bed. The atmosphere was grim. The German wife was terrified of Fred, who was apparently moody to the point of near insanity. Just before we went to bed, the wife took Alyson aside. She tried to tell Alyson a few truths about the home life of a European trophy wife in Iran but scuttled away when she heard Fred moving around. After a horrid night, we slipped out before Fred got up. He was one of the more frightening people I've ever met.

By the time we got to Tabriz, after many hours of driving, we were both again emotionally shattered. It was November 7 and, once out of the sun, it was freezing cold even during the day. Plus we'd had no mail in Tehran. The crown jewels museum was again closed, so I never saw the Peacock Throne.

Without discussing it, we knew that we would drive back to London fairly quickly if we could.

Leaving Alyson, whose Indian fever or flu had flared up, I went out to deal with Elsie's needs. A minor oil leak was fixed in a dubious-looking local garage, but my initial efforts to buy snow chains for the passes in Turkey were futile. I then discovered that they were called Schneeketten in Tabriz, just as they would have been in Munich. Much haggling followed before I bought a used set for 1000 Iranian ryals or about $12. German influence cropped up in unexpected places during the trip, making me suspect that, if Hitler's military attempt to cross the Caucasus and drive on into India in 1942 had succeeded, the Germans might been warmly welcomed, especially in Iran.

On my own, I went to see Chaplin's *The Circus* along with a large, enthusiastic audience. In Tabriz, Chaplin was still the greatest star. The film, a hymn of love to the circuses of Chaplin's youth, touched us all. There was much tearful snuffling and handkerchief work.

Early the next morning, we left Iran with relief. As a final insult, an Iranian border guard insisted that Alyson's passport was a fake. We dug our heels in, told him that we would report him to a great and powerful friend of the Shah, and didn't give him a ryal.

The first snows had come, but the Turkish passes were still clear of snow and as beautiful as I remembered. The mountain views, especially of snow-covered Mt. Ararat, were as stunning. The air was perfect. Alyson perked up. We had the road to ourselves. At around 2300 meters, we saw a frisky red fox. We took this as a sign to stop and walk for an hour in the mountains. We drove on through poplar-filled valleys and cherry orchards whose leaves had turned bright orange.

Alyson in the Turkish Mountains: Elsie the VW Bus in Background

That night we stopped in Erzurum, feeling tired, relieved, and pleased with ourselves. I wrote in my journal: "Blessed Turkey! Iran is shit on toast, though Erzurum at 1950 meters is as cold as anyplace could be. But this hotel is warm and friendly and cheap, and Turkish food a joy. And wine at last!"

———

I am not prone to an instinctive dislike of people individually or collectively or of the places where they live. Travelling is a great joy for me. I would mostly like to go back to places and see more. I am, however, willing to make an exception of Iran. From the Greeks onwards, European observers generally had little good to say about the Persians. For example, the Greeks considered themselves free men and the Persians cringing slaves. Modern Iran is only about 50 percent Farsi-speaking ethnic Persians, the rest being Turks, Baluchis, and Arabs. In 1971, there was still a sprinkling of Christians, Jews, and Baha'i and other miscellaneous minorities, since hounded out of the country. My comments apply only to the Persians—the modern Iranians.

Many travelers sense an undercurrent of hysteria and suspicion in Iranians. Perhaps this is the result of Iranians being Shiites, with the miserable Shiite traditions of pathos, martyrdom, and flagellation. Or perhaps the Iranian wariness is explained by the long Persian experience of foreign conquerors and would-be conquerors, capped by the more recent Anglo-American interference in Iranian affairs. Iranians are so ready to blame the British for anything bad that happens in Iran that there is a famous comic character in modern Iranian literature, Uncle Napoleon, who sees British conspiracies everywhere.

This long history of foreign interference with Iran is indisputable. The importance of Iranian oil guaranteed the far-from-benign twentieth-century involvement in Iranian affairs by the British, the Russians and, more recently, the Americans. Iran was effectively divided during World War II between a Russian zone in the north and a British zone in the south. And the last Shah's father, who had seized power between the two world wars, was deposed in 1941 by the Allies for being pro-Nazi and generally obnoxious.

However, too much is made of the joint Anglo-American, CIA-financed coup in 1953 that toppled Mohammad Mossaddeq, an allegedly democratically elected leader who had nationalized the Iranian oil industry to the rapturous joy of the Iranian masses. (The masses were not aware of the clauses in the Iranian constitution that protected foreign property.)

A little history will illustrate why Mossaddeq was not exactly the people's hero, and why the two Pahlavi Shahs were not as hostile to the broad, long-term interests of the Iranian people as they are now portrayed.

Like Turkey, Egypt, and many other parts of the Middle East, Iran experienced a top-down movement for reform before World War I.

A small, western-educated elite of lawyers, sons of landowners, and their friends wanted to haul Iran into the modern world. In effect, this meant opposing the influence of Islam and the Shiite clerical establishment as much as it meant opposing the weak rule of the then Shah who granted foreign businesses lucrative concessions, especially in connection with tobacco, that caused violent nationalist protests.

A Constitutional Revolution took place in 1906. This was followed the same year by a new constitution that appears to have been modeled on the Belgian constitution, a curious choice. This constitution was liberal in the nineteenth-century European sense. It offered extensive protections for property ownership, not surprising given the strong influence of large landowners, but it restricted the voting franchise severely. Those disenfranchised included: all women, foreigners, everyone under twenty-five, "persons notorious for mischievous opinions," active military personnel, and certain other groups. Obviously, deciding who could vote was subjective and could be locally manipulated.

The constitution established a parliament called the Majlis. Among the requirements for election to the Majlis were a number that offered further scope for manipulation. The candidate had to be fully literate in Persian (in a country of mass illiteracy), an Iranian subject of Iranian descent (in a country that was only about fifty percent "Iranian" in the sense of speaking Farsi and not Baluchi, etc.) and "locally known" (presumably by the local landed gentry). This constitution remained in place, however nominally, until after the ousting of Mossaddeq in 1953.

Ignoring the Constitutional Revolution, Russia and Great Britain formally carved Iran into spheres of influence in 1907. A period of disorder followed, until Reza Pahlavi, head of the Royal Persian Cossack Guard, seized power and cemented his rule by expelling the last legitimate shah in 1925 and crowning himself in his place.

As Shah, Reza Pahlavi was a modernizer and opposed to clerical influence. He built roads, railroads, and factories, made some social improvements, and tried to educate the people—with mixed success due to clerical opposition. He banned women from wearing the chador and opened such universities as there were to women. Equally controversially, the Shah attempted to force men to wear the Pahlavi hat, which looked like the French military kepi. Since the Pahlavi hat had a brim, it interfered with placing the forehead on the prayer mat during Muslim prayers. Europeans took the hat as a joke. Robert Byron said that the hat made the wearer look like a "decayed railway porter."

Reza Shah was tolerant of minorities and even prayed in the ancient synagogue in Isfahan. These policies made him hated by the mullahs and by the landed elite who had controlled the now impotent Majlis. Reza Shah used the Majlis as a rubber stamp for his regime.

After Reza Shah was expelled in 1941 for his pro-Nazi sentiments, he was followed by his son, also Reza, who became known to me initially as the Shit of Iran thanks to *Private Eye*, a British satirical magazine of the 1960s and 1970s. Reza Shah Jr. had the same secular, modernizing approach as his father. Thus, he continued to have problems with the clergy and with the Majlis. For example, he gave women the vote.

Mossaddeq was as bitter an enemy of Shah Jr. as he had been of the senior. From a landed, upper class family, he was educated at the Sorbonne, then took a doctorate in law at Lausanne. Mossaddeq was no ordinary Iranian but the representative of a tiny, tiny secular minority. He tried hard to keep the clergy, who did represent ordinary Iranians, out of politics. Mossadeq was an aristocratic, secular nationalist.

Mossaddeq was elected prime minister by the corrupt Majlis, not by any form of democratic vote. Once in power, Mossaddeq cancelled a series of elections. Furthermore, the CIA coup was made easier by Mossaddeq's custom of retiring to his bed and theatrically and publically weeping for days at a time when things went badly for him. The coup was provoked by Mossaddeq illegally seizing the British-owned oil industry in 1953.

Though this CIA coup has a bad name among the political left or high-minded in both the US and the UK, this reaction is an example of projecting western values onto an alien setting. Not only was the coup fairly bloodless due to much British help in its planning, outside the Banana Republics it was the only completely successful coup the CIA ever managed to pull off. In comparison, think of the unsuccessful Bay of Pigs invasion. Over all, the coup was probably the least bad outcome for literate Iranians, and especially for educated Iranian women.

The Shah was restored. He ruled dictatorially but reasonably effectively until megalomania overtook him. Jimmy Carter pulled the plug on the Shah, who was ailing, in 1979. Carter's predictable do-gooder thinking about Iran was muddle-headed and led to revolution in Iran and the collapse of American influence there. The consequences of overthrowing the Shah were negative for the US then and now. Whether the overthrow of the Shah was good for most Iranians, particularly women, is at least debatable.

Initially, the Iranian economy grew strongly after Mossaddeq was toppled as the price of oil rose, though no one would claim that the benefits were fairly distributed. The middle class was enriched, though average living standards also rose fairly dramatically from a low base. The price was the omnipresence of Savak, illustrated by the water cannons that Alyson and I saw in every little town.

Even disregarding the current electoral manipulation in Iran and the murderous suppression of the opposition, it is hard to accept post-1979 clerically-run Iran as an unqualified improvement over the Shah. Basically, the political possibilities for Iranians during the past hundred years have been dictatorship by a shah, theocratic rule by medieval-minded clerics, or chaos and foreign intervention.

Anyway, neither the 1953 coup nor the repressive behavior of the Shah is sufficient to explain the nature of modern Iranian society or its generalized paranoia. The Iranian people's collective memory is shaped by thousands of years of being continuously mistreated by whoever was in power. Western interventions are merely a recent aggravation.

My impression is that Iranians in practice treat each other as badly as they would like to treat foreigners. They are like some cringing, beaten dog that bites without warning. Or like some Uriah Heep, just waiting for the right moment to give his neighbor a good, swift stab in the back.

Of course, it is profoundly politically incorrect to suggest that there is such a thing as national character, let alone to imply that any nation's character is inherently nastier than any other's. To do so is one step away from—shudder—racism! The mantra must always be that there is nothing wrong with the Iranian people; it's their goldarn leaders. Remove the current shah or clerics or revolutionary leaders, and every Iranian will stop hating Israel – or his neighbor - and promptly get on with a peaceful, happy life. What a fantasy.

It is still just permissible, I believe, to draw inferences about various human societies from clear, factual evidence. To state that most foreign invasions of Afghanistan ended in failure is tolerated, since the historical evidence is hard to refute. To suggest, though, that these defeats were the inevitable result of some enduring and extremely macho features of Afghan culture or that these features weigh heavily against success in plans to democratize Afghanistan within a limited time frame—that is, in less than a century of occupation—is probably not acceptable.

We were delighted to leave Iran. Anyone who thinks that he or she would enjoy a nice long stay in the place should be encouraged to go there at once. And anyone today who thinks that the Iranians are suitable custodians for one or more nuclear bombs has a wire loose or works for the US Department of State.

The Way Home

We moved on to Giresun on the Black Sea. The restaurant we had dinner in was chaotic because it was Ramadan. All the locals descended upon the restaurant at the dot of sundown and gobbled everything in sight. Whatever the mess, it was a fun, friendly place, and there was plenty of food left for us. There was a parrot in a cage munching on sugar lumps, plus two chubby grey partridges, with black-and-white stripes on their wings, running around on the floor. The partridges, utterly tame, wandered under the tables, looking for crumbs and sounding like two tiny old ladies clucking at each other.

The food was marvelous: a ragout of meat, tomatoes, and aubergines, plus steak and salad with lots of red Turkish wine and the wonderful flatbread. After dinner, Alyson tried raki for the first time. "Not delicious," was her verdict, "and looks like alcoholic Milk of Magnesia."

Our host and his friends were huddled together around a large woodstove. Alyson noted that they were chuckling together over a newspaper that featured large photos of plump, semi-naked women, yet their own women in eastern, rural Turkey were often veiled to protect men from temptation. Strange.

Driving in Turkey was a continuous pleasure compared with India or Iran. Apart from the wonderful scenery, we passed groups of school boys dressed in black smocks with a white Eton collar. The girls were more-or-less dressed the same as the boys but had white bows in their dark hair. The farmers were active, getting ready for winter. We saw them plowing with tractors, horses, and oxen. But the sowing of winter wheat was still done by hand. While driving up a hill, a fine, young fox ran across the road in front of us.

We took one look at Ankara, covered by its evening blanket of dense smog from coal fires, and drove straight through to Bolu where we stopped for the night, unable to brave the truck traffic any longer.

We spent three days in Istanbul, recharging ourselves. Alyson loved this city that smelled to her of "tangerines and hot chestnuts." It was cold but we had a happy, interesting time. Alyson was stunned by Santa Sophia to a degree that even I as an agnostic found touching. The mostly whitewashed, austere, museum-like interior of Santa Sophia totally flipped her because she could sense the glories of the Christian past, see the icons and the golden mosaics, smell the incense, and hear the priests chanting.

In the Blue Mosque, she enjoyed watching a grizzled old Turk letting his cute granddaughter run about on the many fine carpets spread all over the floor inside the mosque, making little detours to avoid the pious adult believers face down on their knees. We wandered through the Topkapi and out along the old cobbled streets, noticing the huge American cars still used as jitney taxis carrying many, many passengers. Petrol cost next to nothing in 1971. We took such a taxi and learned that the driver had fought with the Turkish army in Korea. In Istanbul you were never far from the army; MPs were everywhere.

The old, brown, wooden houses along the Bosporus, leaning at odd and unlikely angles, charmed us, as did the overly made-up, westernized Turkish girls in their overly large maxi coats. Ataturk would have been proud of them. At night we walked across the Galatea Bridge and watched ships moving with their bright searchlights scanning the water and the shoreline.

We spent our last night in Turkey in Edirne, which has mosques as fine as Istanbul's. It wasn't much of a night for sleeping because drums in the mosques started a terrific racket at 2:30 a.m. Ramadan was still going on, and pious Muslims had to eat before dawn.

Rushing through Bulgaria—a good country to rush through— and managing to survive driving the length of grim, grey, Communist Yugoslavia on the dangerous Autoput, we arrived in Trieste and back in real Europe. Bulgaria and former Yugoslavia are in a Balkan, not-quite-European, category of their own. It's something to do with eating goat plus having an intense desire to flay your next-door neighbor alive and then nail his skin to your front door.

That night I went to bed feeling sad. The future was once again uncertain, the marvelous journey in some way already over. In the night I had a soul-shaking nightmare that I'd had before and would have again. It was my worst ever.

I was back in New Haven and back at Yale, desperate to graduate and to get away forever from that ghastly city and its hideous mock-gothic university. Finals were upon me! Somehow I was totally unprepared! Especially for French Literature II. *Aidez-moi*! Who the hell was Racine? Did he write *Phaedre*? Or was that Corneille? And what about Rimbaud? What was his connection with Baudelaire? *Bougres jumeux? Quelle mélange horrible. Sauvé qui peut*! My fate was settled; I would fail and be condemned to spend the rest of my life in New Haven. And this was on top of puberty in Cleveland, plus my drunken, psycho parents.

I woke us both with a scream. Alyson was with me in a huge bed in the Grand Hotel de la Ville in downtown Trieste. We cuddled and soon slept. The future couldn't be that awful.

***

We arrived in Geneva. I promptly went to the Union Bank of Switzerland where all my remaining money was supposed to be waiting, telexed from the United States. Just as promptly, an unsmiling Swiss teller told me that there was no money waiting. I watched him go through the telexes methodically and finding nothing. *Rien de tout, monsieur.* I suggested that a small cash advance would be helpful, say, one hundred dollars? The suggestion did produce a small wry smile. But no money.

I called my bank. They said that they would immediately send a telex confirming the transfer. And so they did; they sent a telex confirming the first telex. Yes, the one that had not arrived. Merde alors. The teller told me to return that afternoon.

The answer was of course an expensive, long, boozy lunch. We had cheese fondue, split a bottle of Fendant, an excellent, light, Swiss white wine, then reinforced the wine with a number of shots of Poire Williams, the wonderful Swiss pear schnapps. This left us both giggling, which would not do to face the bank employees. Many cups of coffee followed.

I went back to the Union Bank. No telex. "Monsieur, please return at five," they told me. Which I did. *Encore rien.*

I had twenty Swiss francs left, or enough for two plates of sausages and pommes frites. I became agitated and noisy. I insisted on speaking to someone senior. I was reluctantly ushered up a long, curving flight of stairs. Please bear in mind that I was wearing a distinctly odd, ragged collection of clothes. Alyson and I had no warm clothing. So I was wearing several T-shirts, a sweater, and a smelly Afghan goatskin vest—all over my unspeakable underwear. With hindsight, therefore, I think that the bank behaved not unreasonably.

I was taken in to M. Huppi, a colorless man with rimless specs and a cool manner. He sat behind a vast desk that suggested he could make decisions. M. Huppi decided that he would advance me a hundred dollars but felt that it was appropriate for him to retain my passport. We went down to my pal, the smiling teller. As we pulled up in front of the teller's cage, the confirming telex from the United States arrived. Joy? No. It had to be checked. I could have a hundred dollars of it without surrendering my passport though.

I went back to the Hotel Bristol. We spent most of our time there, not just because the weather was cold, but also because we could charge things to our room. Also we felt the cold keenly because we were still suffering from our Indian plagues. As a child, Alyson had been called "Tin Ribs" by her father, but no one had ever suggested that I was skinny. Now we could ping each other's ribs like xylophone keys. We looked like a couple on a poster for a hookworm eradication campaign.

Alyson was in bed, dozing. I stripped and dumped my rags on the floor and got in with her.

"Mmmm," she said. Then she asked, "Do you remember when that friend of yours said that we would want to marry when we came back?"

"Yes."

"Do you want to?"

"Yes."

"Me too…I think."

The next morning I went back to the Union Bank of Switzerland for the cash and on to the Hotel de Ville as soon as it opened to investigate marriage in romantic Geneva. The investigation didn't take long. Getting married, like being broke, was not something that the Genevoise authorities wanted foreigners doing in their city. Weeks of residence, hefty fees, and multiple documents were required. Plus a physical that sounded like that required to join the army. The descendants of John Calvin weren't having any Wassermann Positives getting married in their city. We weren't sure whether we were disappointed about this marital setback. So we had another boozy Fendant-quaffing lunch and decided to see a film, any film.

I bought tickets at the first cinema we came to. Alyson rushed ahead of me into the already darkened theater. She descended right to the front of the theater, where I joined her for a discussion about where to sit. After a bit of shushing from the audience, we turned to go back up to the rear seats. Just at the moment Alyson turned, a drunken Swiss popped up from nowhere, tripped into Alyson, and smashed her nose, starting a massive nosebleed. I called the man an imbecile. He mumbled unpleasant things. I probably should have hit him, but Alyson said to ignore him, shut up, and sit down.

The film was terrible, but neither of us has ever forgotten it. Called *Red Sun*, it starred the great Japanese actor, Toshiro Mifume. For some reason that was completely unclear to me, Mifume was riding around the American West, trying to kill the great French gangster actor, Alain Delon. The plot was utter drivel. Alyson insisted on sitting through every minute of it with my handkerchief stuffed up her nose. The British upper lip remained stiff, whatever the nasal damage. Later, Alyson would say that she married me because I always carried a handkerchief.

The next morning Alyson woke with the curse and a grossly swollen nose. We went to the Geneva municipal clinic for an X-ray. The nose was broken, but there was nothing to do about it. I told her that her new nose reminded me of Capucine in *The Pink Panther*. This did not please Alyson since she believed that Capucine was a man who had a sex change. We had a usefully distracting discussion about this.

November 21 we arrived in Annecy, just across the Swiss border into France. Some years before, Alyson had seen a film, *Claire's Knee*, which was set near Annecy. She had always dreamed of a weekend there in the off season, so off to Annecy we went.

A dream place, set on a lake surrounded by high mountains, Annecy exceeded our expectations. We stayed in what seemed a simple place, one of the few open, and had a splendid meal. Checking the bill, we discovered that the hotel and meal would cost over a hundred dollars. Not only was this a large amount in 1971, it was many times more than we had ever spent in one day on the road, including gasoline, repairs and so forth. That night we slept wonderfully despite the howling gale outside.

The next morning was the true end of the trip, though I didn't realize it until later. It had snowed heavily in the night. To leave Annecy, we had to drive up a long upgrade on a narrow, two-lane road. Elsie started off confidently but, towards the end of the upgrade, our faithful VW balked when the car in front slowed. I tried to reverse down to the bottom, with Alyson directing us, but we skidded into the ditch by the side of the road.

This called for fortification. We walked down to the nearest restaurant. No one was eager to help us, so I had several coffees, then walked back up to Elsie and tried to put on the Iranian chains I had haggled to buy. They were faulty and in pieces. Knowing the Iranians as I did, I should have inspected them carefully in Iran.

However, by putting the chains under the wheels, I got us out of the ditch, and then reversed the rest of the way down to the bottom. By this stage my feet, still encased in the British desert boots I'd worn throughout the trip, were soaked and freezing.

At the bottom, quite a number of vehicles had accumulated, unable to climb the grade. Probably a little cooperation would have freed this pack, but it wasn't the sort of situation that brings out the best in the French. The largest stuck vehicle was a major tractor-trailer with an aggressive French driver. This guy borrowed my folding entrenching tool, threw a lot of dirt and sand under his wheels, put his rig into super-low gear, and blasted his way up the incline with lots of skidding and bashing of stalled cars along the way.

It was only as he drove away that I realized that he had taken the invaluable entrenching tool with him. But the road was now clear for us to make a successful run. And I realized as we drove away that I wouldn't need an entrenching tool again soon. The trip was over.

London and Marriage

L ondon in December 1971 was damp, cool, and grey, just as always, but that year London seemed somehow drained of its usual winter social zip.

We met our friends and tried to explain what we had seen. Their curiosity was restrained; their lives had gone on while we were away. Plus we were out of touch with the theatre, with the hot gossip, and with the London scene in general. Our friends were bright and interesting people with plenty of ambition but not the sort of people who would ever drive to India. Fly to Paris for an unscheduled dirty weekend, yes; go overland to somewhere hot, dirty, and bowel wrenching, no.

We talked in a desultory way about marriage, but the momentum was lost. We were drifting, though living together at 86 Addison Road, Alyson's cheerful-but-eccentric flat. Some problem with the electric wiring made touching the ever damp walls a mildly tingling experience. In the kitchen, though, real caution was essential. Make contact with the sink and the fridge at the same time, and you were instantly aware of your mortality.

———————◆———————

We visited the Honorable Jane at the Priory, London's number-one private hospital for the mentally agitated who needed tough love. Rehab as such didn't exist then. Jane, stretched out in a hospital bed, looked more than ever like someone in a Dachau liberation day photo. We talked aimlessly about travel. Jane still couldn't admit, or even allude to the idea, that not eating was a death sentence. Alyson and I wept when we left Jane. We were sure that we would never see her again.

And we never did. But she made a full recovery, married, and moved to South Africa, where she had a child and pursued a successful career in photo journalism. Happy endings do occur.

———————◆———————

My wheels were spinning. I needed urgently to work, but I couldn't seem to find a job. Alyson and I went to stay for the weekend with the Kershaws in their converted tithe barn in Gloucestershire. They were as warm and funny as ever. As always, I sat up late talking with Barbara and Harry about every possible thing. We went for long walks as usual and watched their two border terriers try to kill any creature that moved. Alyson was accepted as part of the gang without any hesitation. I was happy, but I was not content.

I had changed. Aged twenty-nine, I could not live as a part-time member of the Kershaw family and conduct a love affair with

Alyson at the level of intensity she needed. Alyson wanted me to be purposeful with her and with the world.

The following week we were back in London. On Thursday, December 8, we went to a little local restaurant for lunch. We talked aimlessly about the future.

Over coffee, Alyson suddenly said, "Why not?"

Why not indeed? I went that afternoon to the Registry Office in Kensington. The clerk of the Registrar of Births, Deaths, and Marriages informed me that he would require copies of our birth certificates and passports. We would need two witnesses. The only date available for a number of weeks was 9:30 a.m. on Saturday, December 11. Would that do?

It would. Alyson thought the time was barbaric. However, we both knew without a word of discussion that the time was now, or we would drift apart. Alyson called her ex-boss, Donald Albery, and asked if he would be a witness. Donald was delighted. Not only would he be a witness, but his Japanese mistress (and later wife), Nabuko Morris, would also be a witness. Without more awkward phone calls, we had the necessary two witnesses.

After the nauseating experience of my sister's wedding, allowing my parents anywhere near my wedding was out of the question. Alyson bravely decided that fairness meant excluding her parents as well. She also thought that her financially strained father would welcome offloading a daughter without any expense. Alyson is the middle one of five daughters. So, we told no one of our wedding plans.

The night before the wedding, neither of us slept. Alyson first had a tearful worry about her mother. Then at 4:00 a.m., Alyson heard burglars climbing up the outside wall. Alyson's flat was on the fourth floor at the back of a large old house. I looked out the bedroom window. Like most old British houses there were a few outside drain pipes, but no one was climbing up them; a feat that would have required an Olympic gymnast in any case. I locked the bedroom door, put a chair against it, and tried to go back to sleep.

At 7:30 a.m., December 11, we somehow got out of bed. Instantly we were both ravenous. A quick search produced a half-empty bottle of champagne, which was rather flat, a more-or-less empty jar of peanut butter, and some Rye Vita biscuits, which were rather stale. We toasted each other and wolfed the peanut butter and Rye Vita. Alyson put on a dress with a full skirt and a smart sweater. I put on a blue suit. Our clothes still hung loosely on us after our all-too-successful Indian power diet.

We went to Donald Albery's smart, modern flat. He and Nabuko were up and ready. They primed us with coffee and tried to calm us. Donald was a classic English gentleman of about fifty-five, grey haired and distinguished. He ran a group of London theatres that had been in the Albery family since the Edwardian era. Alyson had been his personal assistant for some years.

Nabuko was a small, beautiful Japanese lady of multiple talents that ranged from playing the piano at concert standard to speaking accented but perfect English and running an international show business agency. She had gotten to know Donald, whose marriage had broken up, through buying the rights to transfer his London plays to Tokyo.

By this time I was incapable of saying my name clearly, let alone driving, so Donald fortunately had arranged a car and driver. We went to the registry office. This office was in an Edwardian stone house on Marlows Road, directly behind Barkers, the Edwardian department store, on Kensington High Street.

Inside the registry office, we were directed to go upstairs. The interior was furnished by the Ministry of Works to a pleasant standard that included wallpaper, wooden furniture, and carpets but was clearly a grade or two below having paintings or objects loaned from the national collections.

At the top of the stairs, the registrar greeted us and ushered us into the wedding room. "Before proceeding," he said, "would you please look at the documents and make sure there are no errors." I looked at them since Alyson was more than slightly dazed by what was happening. Donald and Nabuko stood behind us.

"There does seem to be a small technical error," I said.

The documents identified us as Mohammed Abdul Rahman and his bride-to-be, Fatima. The registrar was more amused by this than we were. He told us to go back downstairs. On the way down the stairs we passed a small, handsome Malaysian man and a small, pretty Malaysian woman coming up the stairs. They too looked bemused.

Downstairs, we were escorted into an identical room. This time the paperwork was perfect, though Alyson vocally resented being referred to in the document as a spinster. The registrar read us a firmly worded statement, saying that marriage was a serious matter and of concern to Her Majesty's Government. Did we understand what we were doing? Each of us in turn said that we did. Then we signed a document, followed by Donald and Nabuko.

We were married.

On our way out of the building, a nicely dressed man offered to take our picture. We gave him our address and a five-pound note. He adjusted a large, old-fashioned camera and took several shots. That was the last we ever heard of the photo. Donald and Nabuko then took us to the Dorchester Hotel for a bang-up British breakfast. We were starving again, so we scarfed up bacon, sausages, scrambled eggs, toast—the works. This was a long time before Alyson decided that meat is evil.

After breakfast, we parted from Donald and Nabuko, who had been exceptionally kind and thoughtful. Not knowing quite what to do with ourselves, we went to the Tate Gallery. We looked in awe, hand in hand, at Stanley Spencer's enormous canvas of *The Resurrection* in which all the dead local Surrey friends and neighbors of the great painter arise from their tombs in Cookham's parish church graveyard.

It was still early. We felt that something was lacking. A ring! We had to have a ring! We rushed to Richard Ogden, a famous ring shop in the Burlington Arcade. They had dozens of styles but fortunately were just about to close, so Alyson had to make a snap decision. She picked a wide gold band that fitted then but became a bore as she regained some of the weight she had lost.

We went back to her flat. Lying around, we realized that we had to tell Alyson's parents. When Alyson phoned them, they were utterly unconcerned, even though they barely knew me. Then I called my parents. My mother answered, sounding reasonably sober, so I wasted no time.

"Mother, I just got married."

"That's nice dear. One of your little surprises. What's the bride's family name?"

This stumped me for a second. "Oh, Vero."

"O'Vero? Are they Irish?"

My mother was a seething mass of barely camouflaged prejudices. What she meant was, "Is the bride a Catholic?"

"No, mother, Alyson is an English Protestant."

"What is her family name?" repeated mother, suspiciously. She wasn't going to let go of this one easily. No female Papist was going to slip into the family without her knowledge.

Right, I thought, let's end this nonsense now.

"V as in vagina, e as in erotic, r as in rapture, and o as in orgasm. Got it?"

———◆———

So began our married life. Long may it continue.

Afghan Holiday 2009

Camel Train near Mazar-e-Sharif 2009:
Unchanging Afghanistan

Some men seek to recapture their past through writing novels in cork-lined rooms. Others prefer Viagra. Travel works for me. My past involved much rough travel in difficult places. Travel makes me feel that life still offers excitement and rich possibilities.

Over the past year, based upon journals, photos, letters, and memory, I wrote the first part of this book, the story of my drive from London to India and back in 1971. That story is not just a hippie trail adventure of eastern roads, gut problems, and broken shock absorbers, but a tale of love and fate.

But Alyson's and my adventure was long ago, now part of our shared past, a tale to tell our children and grandchildren and perhaps a reminder for today's virtual-reality explorers that the real world can be as exciting to explore as worlds in hyperspace.

Of course, the countries we passed through on the long drive remain much in the news. Especially Afghanistan. I often thought about the Afghans I had met in 1971 and about their shockingly dramatic, dangerous, beautiful country. The Afghans have gone through a long and terrible collective martyrdom since then. That year was one of the rare, peaceful interludes in Afghanistan's long and bloody history. I sometimes wondered what I might find in Afghanistan today. I read whatever came out about Afghanistan, sometimes mentally querying newspaper pieces that I was certain were factually wrong. But I had no plan to go back.

By a fluke, at a summertime dinner party, I met a retired British ambassador to Russia, a man considerably older than I, but lively and full of stories about the agonies experienced by the Soviets in their Afghan struggle with the mujaheddin. The ambassador had recently been in Afghanistan. He e-mailed me a journal of his travels. Travelling within the country was possible!

Impulsively and instantly, I decided to go back. I did not share this decision immediately with my family. I didn't want to overexcite anyone until I found out whether it was practical for a middle-aged American tourist to go to a place where a lively insurrection against American-led forces was ongoing.

Preparing a justification for going, I rationalized my decision to go as necessary to round off my travel saga. Some sort of closure to the story was needed. Also, I wanted to see for myself if there was the slightest justification for the United States to stay in Afghanistan.

Adding what I remembered of the rugged Afghan terrain (and of the even more rugged Afghan people) to my vivid recollection of coming home as a young soldier from Vietnam, I doubted the willingness of the fickle American public to remain focused on what was certain to be a long, frustrating struggle. The global policeman role simply doesn't work for America; there is always another Super Bowl to distract us. But, perhaps it really was different this time? Was it possible that an American military intervention might actually do more good than harm? Why not see for myself?

My main concern about going was not the fighting. Though grim for the military participants, the Afghan "insurrection" is not a war and didn't much worry me. Six thousand American soldiers were killed during the year I spent in Vietnam as a soldier. As of February 2012, about 1700 American soldiers were killed in Afghanistan since we started chasing Osama bin Laden in 2001 or around 150 a year. That is less than the annual murder rate in Washington DC.

I would simply avoid American soldiers like the plague and, as in visiting our nation's capitol, hope that I wasn't caught in the equivalent of some crack dealer's crossfire. After all, Afghanistan is much larger than Washington DC. No, my main concern was a fear of humiliation, of being exposed as an overage, posturing idiot. There was no point in babbling about going to a place that many Americans, however wrongly, consider as dangerous as Omaha Beach on D-Day only to find that I couldn't even get an Afghan visa or medical insurance. Without a visa, going is impossible. Without medical insurance, such a trip is selfish folly.

Naturally, I ignored the usual US Department of State warning against going to Afghanistan. Long ago, as an emerging markets investor, I learned that the last people to know what is really going on in a strife-ridden, third world country work for the US Department of State. Buying a local banker a drink, talking to people you meet in the street, and generally keeping your ears open is a far better use of research time than going to an US embassy briefing.

With occasional honorable exceptions, State Department employees resist assignments to "dangerous" countries, believe their own warnings about possible threats, and in consequence lurk within their fortress-like embassies and compounds. British Foreign Service people are much better informed as a rule and are more apt to be found out in the bush. And middle-aged French travelers are often even better sources of information.

To be fair, the bureaucratically busy employees also don't want to have visiting American tourists getting their asses shot off. That leads to lots of boring paperwork in order to have the body shipped home.

Since it was already September, I had to move fast to fit my trip in before the winter. I bought the *Lonely Planet Guide to Afghanistan*. This guide is essential for traveling in Afghanistan. It includes the best short history of modern Afghanistan that I have read and essential general information about traveling around the country. Afghanistan is either radically too hot or miserably too cold for even moderately enjoyable traveling most of the year. Searing heat everywhere makes travel draining in the summer. Twelve-thousand-foot high passes can be closed suddenly by snow or avalanche in the winter. Spring or fall are the only rational times to go.

The *Lonely Planet Guide* listed two companies that organized travel within Afghanistan. I e-mailed both pronto. Within a day, Rebecca of Great Game Travel replied. The other company never answered my e-mail. In any case, I would have chosen Great Game merely for their Kiplingesque name, but Rebecca quickly proved helpful and competent.

Great Game Travel's suggested itinerary had me enter Afghanistan from the north via Uzbekistan. Using the same invasion route as the Soviets, I would cross the Friendship Bridge over the Oxus or Amu Darya River and enter via Mazar-e-Sharif.

This sounded perfect; I hadn't visited Mazar in 1971. I had always wanted to see buz kashi, the Afghan form of polo, played with the headless carcass of a goat. Buz kashi is a Mazar specialty. Great Game asked to be paid in advance, using a bank transfer. The price quoted for a two-week tour with guide and vehicle was a fraction of the cost of going to a golf resort in Florida for a few days.

My trip was off to a good start until I went to the Uzbekistan consulate in New York City. I had downloaded some rather confusing Uzbek visa forms. I obtained a US postal money order for the stated visa fee of forty dollars. Cash, checks, or credit cards were unwelcome. The visa process seemed rather opaque but it was a long time since I had applied for a central Asian visa; before Uzbekistan became a country, in fact. So I went with the flow. The Uzbek consulate phone message was brief and useless, and the only office extension was always busy. It seemed best to go into the city and apply in person.

The public part of the Uzbek consulate is one small room furnished like the waiting room of a down-market podiatrist. One wall featured a small, dark, European-looking male clerk behind a pane of bullet proof glass with a small slot for documents at the bottom.

Standing aggressively in front of the glass was a forceful, athletic, dyed-blond woman in a black dress, wearing many bracelets and multiple earrings of that real but too reddish gold sold in the Dubai Airport gold market. The woman was neither wholly European nor Asian; her features were hard to place. Behind the woman in black was a small, silent, much younger Central Asian woman with jet black, long straight hair and an absolutely flat, pale bronze colored face. The face of the younger woman was so flat that it looked as though someone had put a large steel plate on it, with a small hole for her small nose, and hammered out all her facial contours by beating on the plate with a heavy hammer.

It appeared that the woman in black was representing the younger woman. The woman in black held some papers in her hand. She was screaming at the clerk behind the bullet proof glass. Some of the screaming was in Russian. Some was in a language that I had never heard before. She threw in an occasional English word like "bastard." Her manner alternated abruptly between the merely threatening to the down-right deranged.

Two young men were standing in line behind the two women. The young guys looked back at me blankly when I got in line and looked quizzically at them. I assumed that some sort of crisis was occurring. This was a misunderstanding on my part.

This drama, it soon became clear, would run and run. The papers the woman was holding were shoved in through the opening in the bullet proof glass. The clerk took them away for some time, then returned and thrust them back wordlessly through the opening. This was repeated a number of times with what looked like exactly the same documents. The woman screamed continuously. She had great lungs. This went on and on.

Finally she stepped aside, pulling the younger woman with her. They sat down at a low table and examined minutely the wad of papers. The two young men stepped forward and jointly presented a one page document. The clerk took it through the opening, looked at it for ten seconds and thrust it back without a word. And, wordlessly, the two guys left. It was an hour or so after I had walked into the office.

I moved up to the window, put my passport, postal money order, and visa application through the window and prepared myself for a lengthy session. But no. My documents came back at once. I would not get a visa that day. Or, it was soon apparent, on any other day. The reasons given were my lack of an Afghan visa plus not having a money order in the exact amount of $197.

"I only want a transit visa," I said. "I will get an Afghan visa later, but surely I don't need an Afghan visa just to enter Uzbekistan and leave the same day? Also, your website said that a transit visa was only forty dollars."

The official's hand waved these comments away. Somehow and without many words, he communicated that these were merely the Wednesday objections. On another day, say, Thursday, other objections might apply. The price of the visa might vary. My photo, or my face, might be the wrong size or shape. Mailing the documents back to me might prove impossible. I left.

Back in rural Connecticut, I e-mailed Rebecca at Great Game Travel, telling her that I could not get an Uzbek visa. I had also learned that my international bank in the UK would not make a money transfer to Afghanistan. In their small-minded, banker's way, Barclays claimed that Afghanistan did not have a banking system that they trusted with client funds. Since I knew that my little local bank in Connecticut, though competent and the oldest in the state, did not make foreign transfers under any circumstances—unless you considered a transfer to the First National Bank of Brattleboro Vermont as foreign—I was stuck.

Rebecca, whom I was beginning to consider a pal, e-mailed me back promptly that the Uzbeks had heads of the purest, hardest granite and had always hated Afghans. If the Uzbeks didn't want me to have a visa, I would not get one. I should get an Afghan visa and simply fly to Kabul and be met there at the airport. As for payment, I could just bring cash in dollars; they trusted me. Credit cards generally did not work in Afghanistan.

Once again, I drove into New York. I went into the Afghan consulate and received my visa in minutes. A smiling Afghan said that tourists were most welcome in Afghanistan. By this time, Alyson realized that I was serious. She became quiet and solicitous about me. After our thirty-nine years of rubbing along together, this unfamiliar concern came as a surprise, though I loved every minute of it.

Hard-minded commercial organizations didn't seem to consider what I was doing as very risky. I bought a special life insurance policy which didn't cost much, given my age. Medical cover with a million dollars of complete medevac cover only cost fifty-nine dollars for two weeks. I am healthy. My son wanted me to get insurance cover against kidnapping. This, though, was prohibitively expensive, so I ignored it.

My middle daughter's boyfriend called unexpectedly the evening before I left. He is a charming, thoughtful young man who played varsity football for Cornell and is now an expert in using statistical economics in marketing. He jolted me by asking with exquisite tact if I would grant him Miranda's hand in marriage before I left, just in case I had a close encounter with an improvised explosive device.

"Of course," I said, "but this is really only between you and Miranda, isn't it?"

"No."

My now son-in-law is a traditionalist; the father of the bride's approval was required. I gave it happily. I felt highly flattered and 104 years old.

Equipped with an extra pair of trousers, insect repellent, sun cream and my Afghan visa, the next morning I flew off to the Afghan insurgency with five thousand dollars in cash—four thousand for Great Game Travel and one thousand for whatever expenses might arise—in used fifty-dollar bills. I put most of the bills in an old money belt that formed a hard lump behind my back no matter where the belt was placed initially. The rest I stuffed in the top of my right sock. I also took some Cipro, plenty of Imodium, and two bottles of Pepto-Bismol. I hadn't been in Central Asia for a long, long time but there are things you don't forget about a place.

The flight to Kabul was long. Very, very long. The first thirteen hours from New York to Dubai on Emirates were about as good as economy flying can be. Emirates have good seats and good food, even in steerage. And the three hours from Dubai to Delhi on Emirates was also good, though the noise level on the plane rose dramatically as we took on a large number of Indian expatriates, homeward bound because they were recently laid off but still happy to be going home.

Delhi Airport appeared unchanged from my last visit in 1971. Still dirty and still a downer, though possibly 3:00 a.m. in the transit lounge, where I was told to wait, is not the right time to revisit Delhi Airport. I sat staring at the dirty floor and dirty walls. After some time, a nice man in uniform came and took away my passport and my ticket for Kabul. I waited and thought "dark night of the soul" thoughts.

After several hours, a different nice man came back with my passport and ticket. He smiled politely but all was not as it should be. Together, we both looked hard at my Afghan visa. Though most courteous, he was deeply suspicious of the visa. I explained carefully and in detail that I was a bona fide tourist, not involved with the NATO forces or planning to do good works for the UN or even for some NGO (non-governmental organization). I was not a terrorist or a CIA man either. Just a tourist.

The background music featured someone playing "500 Miles," on what sounded like a recorder. Over and over.

Finally, I was allowed to go through security and then promptly sent back. I'd passed the metal detector and the bag X-ray, but my hand luggage did not have a cabin baggage tag on it. It was essential to have such a tag for yet another nice man in uniform to stamp. I went as instructed to the information desk where the only available tag was for Air Ethiopia. Nonetheless, this tag was accepted and then properly stamped.

On October 5, 2009, I arrived in Kabul Airport. I'd been told that Hamid of Great Game Travel would meet me but hadn't understood that no one but passengers could enter the small, chaotic terminal. After borrowing a cell phone from a new pal, I found that Hamid and a driver were waiting in the car park outside the airport. There were well-armed Afghan soldiers milling around and a number of checkpoints, but overall it wasn't like the bowel-chilling uncertainty of arriving as a soldier at Ton Son Nhut Airport in Saigon in 1966.

Hamid was a black-haired, good looking, bright twenty-one-year-old college student who spoke fluent English. He was wearing a dazzling orange payraan tombaan. The payraan is a loose, long shirt worn over the tombaan, or trousers. The outfit is traditional; the color orange is not. Hamid was making a youthful fashion statement to stand out from the crowd, one that would have earned him a savage beating from the Taliban a few years earlier.

At college, he was studying English and American literature. Hamid had just read and enjoyed *Billy Budd*, which impressed me. Melville is uphill work. Hamid's family had been refugees in Iran and Pakistan, but he had an upbeat attitude and was optimistic about his own future. He hoped to win a scholarship to study in the United States or England. Hamid had not yet read *Kim*, so I urged him to, if only to know the origin of the Great Game.

Hamid planned to take me up into the hills for a picnic. He was all for going at once, but I insisted upon going to the Great Game office to get rid of the cash I was carrying. Plus, I wanted to be sure that the company really existed; they seemed so remarkably trusting. No problem; the Great Game office was in a secure private house and even had a flush toilet.

The first thing I noticed in Afghanistan is that the population has exploded. Kabul especially has ballooned in size since 1971. Five million people are thought to live there now, drawn by better security than in the countryside and by at least some hope for a better life. No one really knows the population of Kabul anymore than anyone really knows the exact population of Afghanistan. Despite having had an estimated one and a half million people killed in the wars, the population has grown dramatically since the last census in 1979. Then, the fixed population was thirteen million plus an estimated two million nomads.

Currently the population is estimated at thirty-three million; this is not a surprise given that each Afghan woman is thought to average seven children. Even a life expectancy of only forty-five years cannot offset such a birth rate. Currently two-thirds of all Afghans are illiterate. Journalists always mention the illiteracy but seldom the high birth rate of the country. This may be because few current journalists remember Afghanistan before the population boomed.

Some projections suggest that there will be over fifty million Afghans within a few decades. Many of these will be illiterate young men who will be unemployed and unemployable, and so unable to marry. This is not a formula for peace in a country where such men are born into a family tradition that stresses honor and the accurate use of small arms. It is, however, a demographic formula that is repeated across much of the Muslim ummah, or global Muslim community.

This Islamic demographic crisis explains why the Taliban find recruiting so easy. It is not only more rewarding emotionally to be a jihadist and defender of the faith than an illiterate and penniless young Pashtun bum, standing around in the dusty streets of Kandahar, but also jihadists get paid in cash, more cash than they would be paid as an Afghan soldier or street peddler.

Western military interventions on the soil of Muslim countries by foreign unbelievers further ratifies the desire of many young Muslim men, pious or not, to join in jihad, to hit back at a world that frustrates them in ways that they can't understand.

Rocket attacks from drones are unlikely to defuse a collective rage that is due in large part to poverty and demographics. However, if we could just airdrop enough Planned Parenthood field workers from a high altitude onto the Muslim world, it might do something to change the situation.

***

Our driver skillfully bulled his way through the awful traffic with the massive bulk of the Nissan SUV. There were cars everywhere, even though a tired used Toyota cost fifteen thousand dollars, according to Hamid. All the cars we saw were used and all came from Canada or the US, paid for somehow by "leakage" from the streams of aid and military support provided by American and European taxpayers. (The average annual family income in Afghanistan is around five hundred dollars.) Fifteen thousand dollars is also the cost of a basic wedding. This aspect of Afghan culture worried Hamid greatly, since the groom's family pays for the wedding.

The driver obviously understood some English and was following our conversation. Speaking Dari with Hamid translating, the driver volunteered that a good AK-47 cost four hundred dollars. Damn! I'd bought one in Vietnam as a souvenir but abandoned it when leaving. And no one had inspected my duffle bag after all.

Hamid stopped to buy Pringles, bottled water, and peanut butter at a mini-supermarket that specialized in foreign foods. Afghans are crazy about Pringles. I saw empty Pringles cans everywhere. Our driver munched them by the handful as we drove. Hamid and the driver were amazed that I didn't share their enthusiasm. The salt and vinegar flavor was their favorite.

There are a few overhead traffic lights in Kabul but none was working. There are no road signs. Apart from the scores of Toyotas, there were brightly painted trucks and old German buses that still had beer ads in German on their sides. Hummers with machine guns on top, manned by Afghans wearing camouflage uniforms and US helmets, were stationed at traffic circles. Motorcycles weaved in and out of the traffic, as did oblivious bicyclists and pedestrians.

I recognized nothing in Kabul. The city I'd known had broad, tree-lined avenues, slab-sided buildings of Soviet-style architecture and goose-stepping Afghan soldiers in grey, wearing Soviet-style helmets. That city had vanished, as pulverized by war as Berlin in 1945. The dust, though, was exactly as I remembered—everywhere and chokingly awful.

We drove north out of Kabul across the fertile river plain. Grapes were spread on well-swept patches of hard-packed ground everywhere, being dried for raisins. Just as I remembered, the hills in the distance were brown, shading into the grey mountains beyond. I saw the first of the big fighting dogs I also remembered from my previous journey.

There were a lot more people around than I expected, including boys with kites. Donkeys were working as hard as ever, pulling wooden carts with old auto wheels. Fine, small horses with a lot of Arab in them stood in the yards of mud-brick houses, idly waiting for their riders with colorful red blankets under their saddles.

As we crossed a dry riverbed, I saw the first of many knocked-out Soviet tanks, still painted light green and not corroded. There was good material in those Soviet weapons. The Soviets couldn't make a reliable refrigerator, but by God they made a fine tank.

Above Istalif, we had our picnic. Hamid had stopped first in the scruffy town of Istalif to pick up some lamb stew with large floating pieces of fat from the fat-tailed sheep Afghans love to eat. I can just about gag it down. But Hamid also bought Afghan naan bread, better than Indian naan bread, because it was so tasty, chewy, tough, sometimes gritty, and generally Afghan in character. And he bought a jar of peanut butter for me. Over the next weeks, I would learn that all Afghans believe that all Americans crave and consume peanut butter on every occasion. Peanut butter does go well with naan.

The picnic site in Istalif was in the garden of a former royal summer palace, now a total ruin. There were large, old pines that must have overlooked the afternoon strolls of the last Afghan king. It was pleasing to imagine the king wandering between them. A spring came out of a bank and trickled down along some of the remaining irrigation channels. It could have been a sad place, but we weren't in a sad mood.

Hamid talked to a ragged boy of about fourteen who apparently slept amidst the twisted girders and stone ruins of the summer palace. What this kid lived on wasn't clear, so Hamid gave him some greasy Afghan banknotes. Afghanistan is awash with orphans and human catastrophes. Travelers should always have some small change.

Before the wars, Istalif had a population of fifty thousand people. It was green, an oasis of sorts; a place where wealthy Kabulis came for the weekend to enjoy the greenery and the abundant water. In the town, the locals made a famous blue pottery. By the time the Soviets were thrown out and the Taliban occupied the area around Istalif, the population had dropped to zero. Istalif became a place of great danger. After our picnic, we visited one of the reasons Istalif had been abandoned. A now abandoned Soviet tank was dug in high above the town for use as a pillbox with its high-velocity gun still pointing down at the road below.

Today, Istalif is back up to a population of thirty thousand, including plenty of Kabulis at the weekend. The blue pottery is again being made, but I turned down the opportunity to buy some. It was attractive but too fragile to lug all over Afghanistan.

That night I stayed at the Heetal Hotel, notable for what then seemed its excellent security. The Heetal was the victim of a car suicide bombing in December 2009 that left part of the bomb-carrying vehicle on the hotel roof. The Heetal is laid out like a midwestern American motel; there were two stories of rooms around several courtyards. My fellow Heetal guests were a mix of serious-looking young females working for NGOs who weren't at all forthcoming, presumably from being hit on once too often, and large, thick-necked men who said casually that they worked in security.

These guys, replete with tattoos everywhere and depressed scars on their close-cropped heads, were quiet and friendly, though not expansive with information such as their last names or what in detail they were doing.

These ex-military types at the Heetal were mostly Eastern Europeans. I discovered this while eating in the simple restaurant at the hotel, run by two Indians and featuring hamburgers and spaghetti bolognaise. We talked across the tables to each other about inconsequential stuff.

⎯⎯◆⎯⎯

The next morning, October 6, I got up early to fly to Mazar-e-Sharif. Mr. Hassan, who would be my guide, met me at the Heetal and went with me to the plane. This was most helpful; the airport security procedures were elaborate, and it was necessary to drag my wheeled bag over a long stretch of gravelly space to reach the first of the many checkpoints.

Mr. Hassan is a Hazara in his late thirties; about five foot nine, with black hair, a suggestion of Asian features, and bronze skin. He was wearing a traditional white outfit with nothing on his slightly balding head. His English was perfect, chatty and colloquial. Mr. Hassan had worked for some time for the International Red Cross during the wars and surprised me several times by saying something in fluent French. He is a natural linguist.

Historically, as readers of *The Kite Runner* will know, Hazaras were low in the Afghan ethnic pecking order. They are Shias and relatively recent arrivals in Afghanistan. Many worked as servants of the dominant Sunni Pashtuns. Whether because of this background or despite it, Mr. Hassan was unfailingly cheerful and friendly with everyone we encountered, regardless of their ethnic origin. Afghans come in a wild variety of shapes, skin colors and sizes but can pigeonhole each other as to religion and ethnic group at a glance.

The flight was uneventful. Afghanistan has a number of private airlines flying to most of the larger cities. The planes are old, but no older and no more uncomfortable than those used for a typical regional economy flight by United or American. The cabin crew are friendlier, though.

I sat next to a young, hejab-wearing American woman. She was blond and bespectacled and had a slight, sexy overbite. She had a Southern accent. She had gone directly from a social work degree at a North Carolina university to work for the Aga Khan Foundation. Just to tease, I asked her if the hejab meant that she was now a believer. "Puh-leeze," she said; she had been harassed into wearing the hejab by her female fellow NGO workers, not by the locals, but she had to admit that wearing it made life easier, and possibly safer, out in the field.

Mr. Hassan and I had a busy day. First, we explored Balkh, a few miles outside Mazar. Called the Mother of Cities, Balkh dates from some 2000 BC. Not much is left. Balkh was not only built of mud brick, but it also had the misfortune to be thoroughly sacked by Genghis Khan. Balkh was Bactra in Greek and hence gave the name to the region of Bactria.

We stood on a high point and imagined what Alexander the Great would have seen, then clambered as high as we could go on a remaining section of city wall. The extent of the walls shows that Balkh covered a large area and must have had a population of half a million or more at its peak. Zoroaster lived and died there some 1000 BC. Later the city was Buddhist and a stopping point on the Silk Route.

Near Balkh, we visited the No Gombad, or Nine-Domed Mosque. This smallish mosque was interesting in itself as possibly the oldest in the country, but even more interesting for me was the shrine by the side of the mosque to a pilgrim who had made the trip to Mecca on foot from the mosque and back seven times during our Middle Ages. This was a heroic achievement, worthy of Marco Polo.

Driving back into Mazar, along the road we saw more fighting dogs, large mastiff-like creatures with scarred faces and ragged ears. As in Kabul, there were no working traffic signals in Mazar despite heavy traffic. And, as in Kabul, the population of Mazar has exploded. It is currently thought to be near two million. So, even if we fail in all other ways, the American invasion, and the resulting corruption-fuelled surge in car imports, will leave a splendid traffic mess behind. We saw a middle-aged man knocked off his bicycle in slow motion at an intersection. People rushed out of shops at once to help him, but he didn't seem to be hurt.

My main disappointment in Mazar was to find that buz kashi (meaning goat grabbing) is only played in the spring. This is a form of polo, traditionally played with a goat carcass. Today a headless calf is used rather than the traditional goat. The horsemen on their ponies try to grab the calf carcass, lift it onto their pony, and ride to the winning spot with it. Afghans today are stronger than their ancestors, and so goats split too easily. Even so, a calf is said to last only for ten minutes or so before a replacement is needed. Not having seen the sport, I can only imagine it. Knives were banned in buz kashi only recently, which suggests the flavor of the game. I liked Mazar; it hums with life.

We went to a traditional carpet shop. Having been burned buying carpets in 1971, I resisted the temptation to buy, but I liked those the young owner showed us. Mazar is a center of rug weaving. Alas, Afghans themselves cannot afford the beautiful handmade carpets and buy in default cheaper machine-made Turkish and Iranian carpets.

To attract a wider buying public, the local makers have adopted some new patterns. I was much taken by a fine carpet showing Jesus on the cross, complete with red wounds, against a grey background. Apart from its pleasing ecumenical originality, the carpet was bound to appeal to Alyson, I thought. It was the perfect size for the floor in front of our widescreen TV. But having no way except cash to pay the three hundred dollars or so it would cost to buy and to ship, I passed on this opportunity.

That night we stayed at the Samir Walid Guest House. With every inch of the floors covered with carpets, we took off our shoes to enter. (Travelers to Afghanistan should be ready to take off their shoes at frequent intervals and not only to enter mosques.) The staff was friendly, and the food was passable. Overall, this guest house had the ambiance and décor of a Red Army officers' club; with massive overstuffed sofas and arm chairs and dangling single overhead light bulbs.

In my room, the ticking of the wall clock advertising Pine Super Slims cigarettes drove me crazy until I took the battery out of it. The exposed electric wires in the bathroom were intimidating, but the flush loo was more than adequate compensation. There are many aspects of the Afghanistan of 1971 that I nostalgically lament, but the demise of the "Persian version," the hole in the floor loo with two cast-iron steps to raise the shoes of the crapper out of the crap, is not one of them.

In the evening we looked at the brilliant green and red lights illuminating the large blue domes of the Shrine and Tomb of Hazrat Ali.

Ali, one of the twelve Shia caliphs, was officially martyred and buried near Najaf in Iraq, but Afghans believe that his body was secretly taken by his followers to Mazar, then a mere town near Balkh. (Mazar means tomb.) Both Shias and Sunnis revere this shrine.

Mazar seemed peaceful when I was there, though there was fighting not far away in Kunduz. Mazar is now controlled by General Atta Muhammad, governor of the province and a Tajik warlord. Atta is a supporter of his fellow Tajik, the wonderfully named Dr. Abdullah Abdullah, who stood against President Karzai, in the probably fraudulent, though American-organized, presidential election.

Previously Mazar, which is ethnically mixed, was controlled by another warlord, General Abdul Rashid Dostum, an Uzbek. Dostum mostly kept the peace in Mazar during the wars but did horrible things elsewhere, such as mindlessly shelling Kabul. General Dostum had a brisk way with the Taliban, which made him popular with Americans. In one case, Dostum is said to have asphyxiated thousands of Taliban prisoners by having them forcefully stuffed into the ubiquitous metal shipping containers that are everywhere in Afghanistan.

There are many of these massive containers in isolated places, yet no one can explain how they got there. With names like NKK or Maersk still on them, the containers are now often used as one room stores, propped up on logs or stones at the back to level them, with the end doors as store front, opening onto the muddy streets of small towns.

The next morning, October 7, we left early to drive to Kabul. Breakfast in Afghanistan has changed since 1971, when all I remember having is bread and honey and green or black tea. Now, boiled eggs, yoghurt, and cream cheese are available everywhere. The cream cheese is usually from Egypt. Peanut butter cropped up again at the guest house.

We drove through the streets of Mazar as the shop fronts were being opened. There were a lot of day laborers standing on street corners, waiting to see if they would get work. If hired, they receive four or five dollars per day.

Driving along, I soon discovered that Mr. Hassan was quite willing to talk about the gut issues in Afghanistan. He was surprisingly open-minded for someone who had lost relatives and been in exile because of his family's ethnic background. Mr. Hassan's family came from a Hazara village along the road to Bamiyan in central Afghanistan. He still had relatives there, but his father had moved to Kabul years before the civil war to work as a plumber.

Mr. Hassan did not blame the Pashtun or any one ethnic group for what had happened. There was abundant blame to share around, though he reminded me that the Pashtun were the only ethnic group that was broken up into tribes and had tribal leaders nursing violent historic vendettas. His theme throughout our tour was that selfishness in one form or other had made it impossible for Afghanistan to function as a nation.

We drove on a straight road through arid wasteland, slowly climbing. The land was barren but not desert. There were occasional mud-walled enclosures of roughly a hundred meters by a hundred meters, set back from the road and used for some sort of seasonal market gardens. At one point we stopped so that I could take a picture of a camel train.

Before taking pictures, we always asked permission. Men always agreed; women, even small female children, always refused. This did not seem to be exactly a religious objection but stemmed from some fear of having the image taken away and misused in some way.

In the wasteland, the only vegetation was low, spiny bushes, often garlanded with windblown plastic bags. We saw boys cutting and gathering the bushes to be used as firewood. Once we saw a large yellow dog running along the road, probably belonging to some out-of-sight shepherd.

Jagged peaks appeared far on the horizon to the right of the road. As the steppe gained in elevation, we drove closer to the mountains and could see faint greens at the base of the brown foothills.

At Samangan, we stopped to see a magnificent Buddhist stupa known by the Afghans as Takht-i-Rustam, or Rustam's Throne. The stupa is carved out of solid rock with panoramic views from the top. Rustam is the mythical national hero of Persia and the subject of Ferdowsi's poetic epic, a sort of Persian Beowulf. For anyone wanting to study this work, Mathew Arnold freely translated part of this poem into Victorian English. Be warned; even the limited part Arnold translated is long and dull.

Under the stupa is a monastery, consisting of a number of caves, used for sleeping, storerooms, and so on. On a beautiful day in October, the stupa was fun to clamber on. In the summer it would be agony to visit, since there is no shade apart from the caves. The site is spectacular, and we had it to ourselves.

We drove on, planning to visit Surkh Kotal, an ancient city, where the legendary King Kanishka caved a giant staircase into the mountain side in the third century AD. However, when we stopped at the local branch of the Ministry of Culture in Pul-I Khomri for Mr. Hassan to obtain the necessary permit for us to visit Surkh Kotal, we were advised firmly not to go.

There is a police post near the top of the mountain where the stairs end. The night before someone had fired an RPG—a rocket propelled grenade—at the police post. Plus, the Pashtun villagers in the village along the small side road up to the site were hostile and might try to kidnap us. This was not the right time for tourists to visit Surkh Kotal.

The culture ministry representative, a small, chain-smoking, middle-aged man with thick glasses, wearing a Western suit, was horribly embarrassed to have to tell us this. The others with him also looked sheepish. The representative smoked nervously and kept looking at the ground. I said to him via Mr. Hassan that I was more than glad to pass up visiting any place that was likely to be on the receiving end of a RPG.

I felt like patting the nervous representative comfortingly upon the head. But instead we milled around for a while, shuffling our feet and looking serious. The culture ministry branch faced a canal or river diversion, stagnant and full of debris. Mr. Hassan and I talked about war and water. Apart from the human catastrophes that have wracked poor Afghanistan, the damage to the ancient but sophisticated irrigation systems that I remembered from 1971 is immense. Fixing the major irrigation systems would be of immense, lasting help to the Afghans.

Dropping our costly obsession with poppy eradication would be another bonus for the Afghans. It would be much more sensible simply to buy the poppy crop and burn it or perhaps air drop it onto Iran. Poppies don't require irrigation, fertilizer, or machinery to cultivate. They are the only feasible serious cash earner in many parts of Afghanistan. Like drug dealing in our American ghettos.

The road started to climb into the mountains. We passed Dowshi, an unimpressive little town, where the difficult road from Bamiyan in central Afghanistan meets the main road between Mazar and Kabul that we were on. I had tried to drive from Bamiyan to Dowshi in 1971 and had failed, with only broken shock absorbers on my VW Bus to show for my efforts.

From this end, the Bamiyan road looked so easy. Driving through Dowshi, I saw a fine little grey male fighting partridge in a bamboo cage, hanging in front of a shop. As well as dog fighting, Afghans like cock fighting and partridge fighting.

We wound our way up to the Salang Pass. On the way the road passes through long, cement-roofed galleries to protect the road from winter snow avalanches. There are no trees or any other obstacles to disrupt the path of an avalanche. (Reforestation is another task the Afghans need immense help with.)

At 3363 meters, or 11,033 feet, the Salang Tunnel was built by the Soviets in the 1950s to create an all-weather link between the north and south of the country and thus expedite the long-planned Russian invasion. Playing their part in the Cold War, the Americans had helpfully built an east–west all-weather road suitable for tanks through the southern part of the country.

To put the Salang Pass into an American perspective, the famous Donner Pass in the western Sierra Nevada is 2160 meters, or 7085 feet. The Sierra Nevada are sometimes mentioned as being like the Afghan mountains, but they are less challenging and heavily forested. The Salang Tunnel is an impressive piece of engineering but a crude one and now needs to be completely rebuilt. The tunnel is 2.6 kilometers, or 1.6 miles, long. There are no lights, and the road surface inside is terrible, with large, broken chunks of pavement and gravel-filled potholes.

The tunnel was built wide enough for two Soviet-era tanks but is a squeeze for today's large trucks. Nonetheless, the massive trucks roar through, going as fast as they can, their headlights dimmed by the thick, exhaust-filled air. Luckily, our Nissan SUV handled the deep, unavoidable potholes far better than my VW Bus would have (though it feels disloyal to mention this).

At the southern end of the Salang Tunnel, the road emerges onto the steeply sloping side of even higher mountains. It was here that some 160 lives were lost in an avalanche in February 2010. The pass has a spooky atmosphere. There was lethal fighting here during the war as attempts were made to block it. I was relieved when we were through it. There have been a number of dreadful accidents in the pass and at least one horrific fire inside the tunnel. For a tourist in the Third World, the most dangerous moments in places like Afghanistan are those spent in a vehicle.

Late in the afternoon, we turned off the main road and entered the Panjshir Valley. We soon passed the marker indicating the furthest point reached by the Taliban in their attempt to take the Panjshir Valley. The Soviet effort, though, penetrated high into the valley. We had already seen numerous abandoned Soviet tanks and guns—Soviet trucks were still in use everywhere—but, as soon as we got into the valley proper, green-painted Soviet war toys were simply everywhere, many with gaping holes where the rocket or shell had pierced them.

Some background history of Afghanistan is necessary not just to understand the Panjshir Valley struggle, but to understand what is going on in Afghanistan today. Nothing is clear and nothing is simple in Afghanistan; the past and the present are muddled up together. Don't be surprised to read conflicting historical interpretations or to learn that allies in one period became enemies soon afterwards. I found the brief historical framework in the *Lonely Planet Guide* useful for getting the chronology straight but the following history is cobbled together from various sources.

For centuries, Afghanistan had kings who ruled from Kabul with varying degrees of authority. All the kings were Pashtuns. Most came to a sudden, violent end, usually through being dispatched by a blood relative.

The first Afghan king, and the effective founder of Afghanistan, was Ahmad Shah Durrani. Before him, western Afghanistan had been a Persian province, and eastern Afghanistan was under the influence of the Moguls. In 1747, the Persian emperor, whom Ahmad Shah served as a cavalry leader, was killed by his own men. Ahmad Shah took the opportunity to seize a great trove of imperial booty and set himself up as king. He was a Popalzai tribal leader, the same tribe as that of President Hamid Karzai today.

After unifying Afghanistan and seizing large parts of the surrounding territories, Ahmad Shah managed to die of natural causes. Few of his royal successors had the same good fortune.

One of the essential books about modern Afghanistan is Rory Stewart's *The Places in Between*. In 2002, right after the fall of the Taliban, Stewart, a former British soldier and diplomat, walked across the mountainous middle of the country from Herat in the west of the country to Kabul in the east. Stewart speaks a number of Afghan languages and was able to appeal to the traditional Afghan rule of hospitality to strangers. He is obviously coolly and madly brave. Stewart likes and understands Afghans and the other peoples of the region.

Of the Afghan rulers in the twentieth century, Stewart notes, "Every Afghan ruler in the 20th century was assassinated, lynched or deposed."

Mohammad Zahir Shah, who may turn out to have been the last ever Afghan king, was still on the throne when we passed through in 1971. Zahir ascended to the throne in 1933 after the traditional unnatural demise of his predecessor. By all accounts, Zahir was an amiable do-nothing. We were aware of his reign only through the numerous photos of the king in public places. But he ruled over a peaceful and unified country, no small achievement in terms of Afghan history. In 1964 Afghanistan actually became at least in name a constitutional democracy.

In 1973 Zahir was deposed peacefully by his cousin and prime minister, Mohammad Daoud, who proclaimed himself president. Daoud continued a policy of playing off the Soviets against the US. The Soviets responded enthusiastically, investing heavily in road projects like the Salang Tunnel and in training the Afghan army. With the Soviets active in the country, what the *Lonely Planet Guide* calls "the embryonic Afghan communists, the People's Democratic Party of

Afghanistan" grew in confidence. In April 1978 communist-inspired soldiers stormed the Presidential Palace and murdered Daoud and his family.

A period of Marxist anarchy followed. An educated, secular (and very small) class of Afghan intellectuals had embraced Marxism without really understanding its broader, explosive implications for a tradition-bound, religious society. Rapid moves to establish women's rights and to secularize society were immediately resented as an assault on the family and on religion and resisted by a large proportion of the population. Always remember that at least two-thirds or more of the Afghan population were then, as they are today, illiterate.

By late 1979, the Soviets realized that the revolution would soon collapse. As in Hungary, the Red Army invaded the country, crossing the Oxus and entering through Mazar-e-Sharif. And, as so often in Eastern Europe, the Soviets set up a new puppet government, having conveniently murdered the previous insufficiently pro-Soviet leader. It appears that the Soviets planned to stay militarily in Afghanistan for only a brief period. However, they profoundly misjudged the forces they had unleashed internally and externally.

Showing an unexpected tenacity after his previous humiliation by Iran, President Jimmy Carter quietly backed the Islamic insurgents against the Soviets. The motives of these rebels were mixed. The leadership of the anti-Soviet jihad was always fragmented, largely divided along ethnic lines. Massoud, for example, was the leader of the Tajiks of the Panjshir Valley in the northeast. Support for the jihad was funneled through the Pakistani secret service, the ISI. Many of the jihad leaders were in exile in Pakistan before the fighting started and had high-level connections in the Pakistani government.

Within Afghanistan, violent political tensions had existed well before the war; Alyson and I had witnessed a nasty riot in Kabul between Islamists and Communists in 1971. After the 1978 Communist coup, the new Communist government murdered many opponents and scared others into exile, creating a permanent opposition.

Osama bin Laden arrived from Saudi Arabia, along with thousands of other "Arab-Afghans." Though all these groups squabbled and sometimes fought among themselves, they fought heroically against the Soviets, who lost control of the countryside. The Americans aided the uprising with money and military equipment, especially Stinger missiles that made it more difficult for the Soviets to use their helicopters effectively. Whether such global, geopolitical strategists as representatives Charlie Wilson or John Murtha had any real understanding of what was going on in Afghanistan is questionable. Hell, fighting "them Commies" was reason enough to back anybody.

The Soviets tried bringing in Muslim soldiers from their Islamic republics, like Uzbekistan. This experiment was a failure, with some Soviet Muslim soldiers deserting to join their local co-religionists. Eventually, after 15,000 Soviet soldiers were killed, Gorbachev threw in the towel. Leaving a Soviet proxy, Najibullah, in political command in Kabul supported by the Afghan army, the Soviets withdrew back across the Oxus in 1989.

The Soviet withdrawal was followed by an unexpected period of relative calm that had similarities with Vietnam after the US pullout. Unexpectedly, Najibullah hung on for some time while the Afghan army supported the government. Several Afghans I talked to remember this period, if not with affection, at least as a time of relative calm. But it could not last.

In early 1992, the mujaheddin surrounded Kabul. The Islamist Pashtun, Hekmatyar, was south of the city. Hekmatyar, an usually evil bastard even by local Islamist standards, was supported by Pakistan and looked like the ultimate conqueror of the country.

However, the previously mentioned Dostum, then an Uzbek general in the Afghan army, led a mutiny in the north that, in the confusion, enabled Massoud to rush into Kabul and occupy the city. This provoked an immediate civil war. Hekmatyar sat outside Kabul and shelled it. Massoud retaliated. Dostum joined Massoud, then switched to Hekmatyar, then went back to the north as a local warlord. Hazara militias were formed. Herat split off under its own warlord.

Ordinary Afghans died by the thousands. And the Americans lost interest. Why wouldn't they? The Soviet Union had collapsed. Afghanistan was "free," or no longer Communist. Good-bye evil empire. America has no real long-term interest in Afghanistan or in Afghans. Like Vietnam, most Americans couldn't spell Afghanistan, let alone find it on a world map. There was no further need to fight to the last Afghan. Or so it seemed then.

War is God's way of teaching Americans geography.
Ambrose Bierce

Enter the Taliban. Whether the Taliban were a semi-spontaneous reaction to the ungodly excesses of the mujaheddin, or were recruited by the Pakistanis as proxies for Pakistani geopolitical interests, or both, they were welcomed by most Afghans who were sick of the civil war and only wanted law and order.

Spreading out from their Pashtun roots in the southeast around Kandahar, the Taliban spread across the country, capturing Kabul in September 1996. Massoud retreated back into the Panjshir Valley. Najibullah was seized from a UN compound and lynched. Women were forced to wear the burqa and banned from working outside their houses. Men were forced to grow beards. Get caught listening to pop music, and you could be publically caned.

Extreme, puritanical interpretations of Islam were imposed on everyone. Women, for example, could be flogged for wearing white shoes, since white is the color of Allah and hence the women were stepping on God. In practice, women could get in serious trouble simply by being alone outside their homes.

And, as had happened so often in Afghan history, the Hazaras, who were Shia, were cruelly mistreated. There were risings in the Hazarajat, the central region of the country around Bamiyan where the Hazara live. Possibly this is part of the reason why the Taliban destroyed the Bamiyan Buddha's, the most famous monuments in the whole country. There are often multiple possible reasons for destructive or cruel behavior in Afghanistan.

Osama bin Laden had a large influence on these developments, though the one-eyed Mullah Omar led the Taliban. Al-Qaeda was disciplined and had proper training areas. The Taliban were a violent religious rabble with many hysterical and petty sub-leaders. Nonetheless, they fought hard.

Massoud succeeded in keeping the Taliban from penetrating the Panjshir Valley. In return for this successful opposition, two suicide bombers succeeded in assassinating Massoud on September 9, 2001. The suicide bombers are generally thought to have worked for the Taliban, but other conspiracy theories abound.

Massoud's death was overshadowed by the events of September 11, 2001, but had a great influence on what followed in the country. Massoud's picture is everywhere. In some ways, the impact of his assassination was like that of Kennedy's; Massoud's image is as powerful in death as in life. Had Massoud lived, the American attempt to reshape Afghanistan might have been more effective, with Massoud in charge as a near dictator. And that would have posed other problems since the Pashtun would never have accepted a Tajik dictator for long. The Tajiks are only twenty to thirty percent of the population and perhaps not as honor driven or blood thirsty as the Pashtuns.

President Karzai, a Pashtun, appears in our press as ineffectual and tolerant of corruption. Bearing in mind that he is as much a tribal leader as a politician, this judgment is probably as unfair as it is unrealistic. Given Afghan history, any tribal leader has to compromise with ethnic realities and with the wishes of his own relatives and clansmen. Plus, the warlords are not going to simply disappear. Some remain powerful locally.

After all, greedy, clannish, venal families are not exactly unknown in American politics. Colonial powers often are quickly disappointed by the puppets they select. The colonial bosses pull on the stings but the puppet doesn't move as expected. The British had this problem over and over again. As did the Soviets.

In any case, the period after the American invasion in 2002 was marked by ups and downs in security and reconstruction that persist until now. Some progress was made: many exiles returned, and the pervasive corruption allowed useful dollars to leak out into the local economy. Kabul was rebuilt from total ruin.

But the core problem remains. Afghanistan is not a country in our sense; it is an attitude; a collection of ethnic groups with powerful shared customs and a feeling of being Afghan in some general way but with no willingness to sacrifice local or ethnic interests to higher national goals.

The post-US-invasion period is examined in Sarah Chayes' *The Punishment of Virtue*. This offers a good explanation of the Pashtun tribal structure and its interaction with the revived Taliban insurrection. It is not a happy read, nor encouraging for anyone who expects a happy ending as the result of US military activities. Like Rory Stewart, Chayes is madly brave, with the added dimension of being an American feminist working in possibly the world's most macho culture.

The Panjshir Valley, which is almost exclusively Tajik, was the epicenter of resistance to first the Soviets and then the Taliban. The Tajiks speak Dari, a Persian dialect, and are instinctively hostile to other ethnic groups. They are Sunni and not organized into tribes like the Pashtuns but identified by their home village or city.

We had turned off the main road to Kabul and onto a good paved road that wound through a series of villages along the road. The road climbed steadily along the Panshir River, through a rural region of small, terraced fields and attached villages.

Night was falling and the air was cold. We planned to stay at the official Tajik guesthouse for important foreign visitors. We had to stop at a number of checkpoints on the road, manned by Afghan Army soldiers who were all Tajiks. Each time, Mr. Hassan had to show documents and give a long explanation of who we were and where we were going. His Hazara face did not fit.

Mr. Hassan resented these checkpoints, repeatedly noting that the Tajiks were selfish and had no sense of belonging to the Afghan nation. He noted that the next valley off to the east was a Hazara valley that welcomed travelers, but Hazaras were not welcome in the Panjshir Valley. Whether Tajiks would be welcome in the Hazara valley was a delicate question that I did not ask.

We passed the tomb of Massoud, the Lion of Panjshir. I wanted to stop, but Mr. Sakhi said that we would come back to it. The tomb sits dramatically on the end of a massive rock outcropping that juts out onto a steep sided terrace above the valley.

Past the tomb of Massoud, near Asteneh, we turned left up a narrow dirt road that wound in dramatic switchback turns up the side of a mountain. At the top was an Afghan Army (but all the soldiers were Tajik) military intelligence outpost. This was obviously a place for spying on whatever happened in the Panjshir Valley. You could see for miles, even in the twilight, up and down the valley, watching the road traffic and the course of the river. Higher up the mountain was an electronic listening post.

At the military intelligence outpost, we were informed that we had the wrong papers. We were sent back to the nearest police barracks. There Mr. Hassan performed a dramatic bit of agitated discussion. Eventually we were off again. We turned again up the same dirt road that led to the military intelligence outpost but turned off it about halfway up to where the guest house was located. Anyone staying there would be under close watch from the intelligence folks. In the gloom we approached the guest house. Not a light was showing in the house.

Standing on the walk in front of the one story guest house were five Tajiks. These ranged in age from twenty to sixty and were dressed in kit ranging from T-shirts, though it was bitterly cold, to traditional Afghan. The elder ones had beards. The younger ones had cell phones. All were smoking; one was smoking a joint. None greeted us. We were not welcome.

A long argument followed, with frequent cell phone calls punctuating the shouting. It appeared that the senior policeman at the police barracks had given us the right to stay, confirming the arrangements Great Game Travel had made, but that the local staff either didn't believe that this policeman was kosher or thought that we were suspicious characters who had fooled some stupid policeman. Things were vaguely menacing. I didn't feel like interrupting Mr. Hassan, who was dealing with simultaneous shouted comments from all the locals.

Finally, we were let into the pitch-dark building. I found my way to what I took to be my room with a small pocket LED flashlight—essential for travel in Afghanistan. In another room, the argument continued. Now the argument was about the cost of running the generator. Mr. Hassan said that Great Game had already paid for this. Eventually a compromise was reached. The lights came on. Dinner would be ready in an hour. What the lights revealed was quite surprising.

Any state visitor would have assumed that his social status had been checked out and found to be severely wanting. The décor was bizarre. The intention was plainly to create something like a film set for a Bollywood epic with vivid yellows and reds on walls and furniture, many colorful rugs, large and small, and lots of massive carved and gilded wooden chairs with red, floral cloth on the seats. The ceiling was painted in glossy white enamel. Everything was brand spanking new but already trashed comprehensively. Some wall lights worked because they had light bulbs; some didn't despite having bulbs. Some fittings hung from the walls by the electric wires.

Most of the working bulbs in my room were brothel red. I took some clear bulbs from a corridor chandelier to replace them. But, yes! There was a bathroom. The brand new bathtub was horribly chipped and had holes in its sides where handles should have been attached. It was filthy, with thick, black grease all over it. The hand basin was precarious to use because it hadn't been fixed to the wall. A heavy mirror rested casually on the wobbly hand basin. But what kind of wussie would want to take a bath in the Panjshir Valley? There was plenty of ice cold running water with which to splash yourself clean.

Actually, the only thing that bothered me at all was the penetrating smell. I am not sensitive to smells, as Alyson can vouch, but this was beyond pungent. It was a penetrating mixture of stinks: still-damp paint; hashish; plenty of fresh human crap, and diesel fumes from the generator. Otherwise, I felt totally content.

Waking early enough to see the light dawning on the top of the mountains on the other side of the valley, across the Panjshir River, thrilled me. One of Alexander the Great's generals might have watched precisely the same view.

We set off early. Back on the main road, we wound our way upwards towards the head of the Valley. We passed through villages, then the paving abruptly ended. We passed farms that operated as they had since the beginning of time. The fields were small and terraced. The harvest was in and teams of oxen were threshing the wheat. In fields that were already threshed, the wheat was bound in staves. Water was diverted from the river into small irrigation channels. The land was fertile and the farms prosperous. Again, I saw fine small horses with colorful saddle rugs and decorated bits standing in farm yards, waiting for their morning rider.

The Nissan went slowly on the rough road, so I could watch girls playing a traditional game with sticks. Mr. Hassan said that the game was called danda kelak. It is played with a long stick, used as a bat, and a short stick, used as a ball. The short stick lies on the ground until whapped briskly with the long stick so that it flips up into the air. The batter then smacks the short stick with the long stick. While the short stick is in the air, the girl hitter runs as fast as she can towards the goal. Being an Afghan game, part of its appeal was that the whapped stick sometimes caught the batter in the eye.

Poplars were planted in little groves, with irrigation canals winding through them. The leaves were just beginning to turn yellow. We were held up several times by rock falls onto the road but road crews with modern Hitachi crawlers soon cleared the large, broken rocks.

Even high up the valley, there was more evidence of the Soviets: tanks, armored personnel carriers, artillery pieces—all with their smooth coat of green paint still intact and generally in pretty good condition, apart from those that had been hit by shells or rockets. In one village, tank tracks were buried in the road as sleeping policemen.

As we slowly climbed, I asked Mr. Hassan numerous questions that must have bored him rigid but he was unfailingly enthusiastic and polite in his answers. A kilo of lamb at one of the fly-covered open air butchers that we saw cost four dollars. A whole live lamb cost ninety to a hundred dollars. The wonderful bread was a bargain at eight afghani, or twenty cents, apiece.

Wonderful grass, such as we enjoyed in 1971, was still available everywhere, but Mr. Hassan disapproved of its use. Weapons could also be found with little difficulty. Officially, Afghanistan has gun controls. In fact, weapons and ammunition are readily available thanks to the Soviets who had left most of their equipment behind.

Mr. Hassan said that when the Soviets were leaving via the Friendship Bridge across the Oxus and crossing into Uzbekistan, General Boris Gromov, the Soviet commander, went last. In the middle of the bridge, General Gromov got out of his armored personnel carrier, pulled out his automatic pistol, and fired off all its rounds back into Afghanistan. Then the general screamed that, although the Soviets had only been in Afghanistan for ten years, he was delighted that they had left enough weapons for the killing to go on for ten times ten years. This story is not confirmed in Western newspapers but is believed by every Afghan I talked with.

Small springs came out of the hillside above the road and ran across it. We reached Parigozar, which means "the Place of the Fairies." There was not much to this village, just simple low huts. Eric Newby went through it during *A Short Walk in the Hindu Kush*. I doubted that Parigozar had changed much since Newby was there in 1956. However, the village was about to change dramatically.

Above us were mighty snow-capped mountains of five and six thousand meters, but we only had fleeting glimpses of them. And, above Parigozar, we hit the end of the road. A large crew with heavy equipment was cutting a way along the hillside, dynamiting and breaking rocks and crushing them into an all weather road, perfectly suitable for tanks, which will connect Afghanistan with China.

The Chinese are paying for this road, which will thread its way to China through the Wakkan Corridor, skirting Pakistan, India and some of the world's highest mountains. The purpose of the road is certainly not to encourage Chinese tourism, so the Indians are freaked by it. Why we don't use the road or similar sources of tension to play off the Indians against their neighbors is beyond me.

As far as I know, the construction of this road has not been mentioned in the American media. Its existence highlights the role that duplicitous, power-based, Great Game diplomacy could play in keeping Pakistan, India, China, and Russia busy with their own problems in Central Asia. Gutsy diplomacy might speed the process of getting American soldiers out of Afghanistan while encouraging the possibility of less outside interference with Afghan affairs after our departure. The possible permutations in playing India off against China, for example, are limitless.

One objection is that such diplomacy leads to mistrust of those playing such games. True - but no one trusts America anyway.

However high-minded our foreign policy intentions, our unstable domestic politics mean that we are simply too fickle to be trusted over time. This does not, however, preclude giving events a destabilizing nudge from time to time. Whether such "red meat" or "teeth in" diplomacy would appeal to President Obama and Mrs. Clinton is another question.

———

We turned back, parked at the roadside, and walked down the hillside into a grove of poplars to have a picnic. Some of the road crew saw us and asked if they could join us. Our driver spread out a large rug. We set out our bread and cheese and the inevitable peanut butter. Various members of the road crew turned up with grapes and more bread. Soon a dozen of us sat around in a loose circle. We checked a GPS device that read 2744 meters or a fraction over 9000 feet. The air was perfect.

The head of the crew was Zalmin Maihanpoor, a burly guy of about thirty-five with hard, massive hands, In the photograph below, he is holding a cigarette. Zalmin was a droll, friendly character who talked and smoked continuously. One of his crew showed me a handful of PK Russian machine gun bullets. Another wore a belt of twelve-gauge shotgun shells. The weapons were to defend their camp against bandits. The crew were all Tajiks from the Panjshir Valley. People from their own village would not rob them, but those from another village might. As road workers, they were rich by local standards and were paid in cash. Also, their tools were valuable.

Afghan Picnic with Road Builders 2009

Zalmin asked me how many wives and children I had. When I said that I had a fine, healthy wife who looked after me day and night, three grown children, and two grandchildren, my status rose immediately. One of the crew, a splendid fellow with his beard dyed black and the look of a Mormon prophet, quickly claimed to have four wives and fourteen children. Zalmin shouted that he was a liar; the man had one wife and a few children. At that, the man said he was planning to buy another wife, so there.

"Why buy another wife," I asked? "Isn't that a terrific expense?"

"Yes, but my current wife is ugly and old."

Zalmin sneered at this comment. Most modern Afghans have only one wife.

Ian, a Scotsman of about fifty, was travelling with us that day. In the photograph above, Graham has a pained expression. This is because Zalmin has just asked Ian the question about how many wives and children he had. Ian is, I believe, what *Time* used to call to call "a confirmed bachelor." For Ian to give a frank and full answer to the question would have been tricky under the circumstances, so Ian just said that he didn't want a wife. This produced exclamations of amazement all round. Ian had another reason to look glum; he just had the first bout of a familiar Asian travelers' complaint.

After we ate, one of the crew produced a home-made musical instrument made of an old five-liter oil can with holes in it, with a stick poked through the can, and wire strings like a two stringed violin. Phonetically, this instrument is called a ghichak. Played with a crude bow, the guy made pleasant music that the crew sang to. When my turn came, I attempted to teach them "Row, Row, Row Your Boat" as a round. This was not a musical success, but I felt gloriously happy.

I would have loved to have climbed up into the hills to look at the massive mountains that we could only catch glimpses of, but Mr. Hassan warned of land mines. So, we drove back down the valley after lunch. We were soon held up by a rockfall and by the subsequent breakdown of the Hitachi digger that was needed to clear the rockfall.

While we waited, I met and shook hands with a fair-haired road worker whose blue eyes and pale skin reminded me of a banker I'd known in Copenhagen. We noticed many fair-haired men and boys in the valley. One theory is that these are descendants of Alexander the Great's men. My theory is that they are the descendants of a particularly active and virile German travelling salesman of the 1890s.

We were held up again by a stubborn Afghan cow that blocked a ford in the river. Animals in Afghanistan have the same forceful character as the people. I thought of the French saying, "This animal is dangerous; if you attack it, it defends itself." None of us felt like approaching the tough-looking animal and slapping her on the bum. We just waited until she moved.

Animals for some reason are not named in Afghanistan. A dog is just "Dog." Mr. Hassan had some terrible scars on his legs from a fierce dog that belonged to his brother-in-law. Therefore, he is not a dog lover. Most Afghans appear to like dogs, despite dogs being considered an unclean beast in Islam.

On the way back to Kabul, apart from going through all the checkpoints again, we stopped at the dramatic tomb of Massoud. We parked by a splendid collection of Soviet war gear, including an anti-aircraft gun that had been used on ground targets as the Germans used their 88 mm flak guns in World War II. Among the guns and tanks were many large photos of Massoud, taken over many years by a French guy who had trailed Massoud everywhere. The tomb itself is stark and impressive and, like the ack-ack gun, commands the valley as far as you can see. It's worth a visit.

Our driver, Mohsen, had Grieg's "Hall of the Mountain King" as his cell phone's ring tone. Disconcertingly, the phone rang a lot.

I noticed that most houses had satellite dishes. There were small water turbines in the river to provide electric power. The fierce Tajik warriors of the upper Panjshir Valley spend their spare time watching pirated Bollywood and Hollywood epics. We stopped briefly for Mr. Sakhi to buy me a beige pakol, the flat, woolen roll-down hat Massoud always wore. Mr. Sakhi did this without my requesting it simply because I had expressed admiration for these hats.

On the way into Kabul, Mr. Hassan described his experience of the Taliban. The Taliban were instantly recognizable by their black turbans and full beards. This was fortunate because all rational people tried to avoid them. Encounters with their brutal horrors were, however, inescapable.

Mr. Hassan had once decided to risk going to a soccer match in the national stadium in Kabul. He went in with friends and had just taken his seat when an announcement was made that there would be a demonstration of the power of Allah before the match began. The exits were then locked. A Taliban leader with a microphone came out into the middle of the large stadium. This announcer talked the audience through the set piece execution of a murderer.

The murderer killed a man with a knife and was caught immediately. The son of the murder victim was sent for and returned from Germany. Mr. Hassan said that the son was an ordinary-looking Afghan who stood in a casual sort of way next to the Taliban announcer. It seemed that the son had gone to the prison, planning to offer Islamic forgiveness to the murderer. Instead of accepting this offer, the murderer made the helpful comment that, if the son had been present, it would have pleased the murderer greatly to have killed him too. This led to the son being in the stadium, ready for action.

Islamic custom says that the weapon used in revenge should be the same as that used in the crime. The Taliban announcer accordingly handed the son a large, curved-blade knife. Without to-do, the son first stabbed the murderer in the throat, and then hacked him to death. With no hesitation, the son ritually washed his hands in the murderer's blood. The Taliban announcer said that Allah's will was done and that the soccer match would commence. The crowd was silent throughout. Mr. Hassan is a gentle man. Telling this horrid tale shook him. I thought that he might weep, but he just turned away and looked out the window of the Nissan.

Back at the Heetal Hotel, I met more mercenaries. One was a chunky Belgian of about forty with multiple tattoos and a pleasant little half-smile that I hoped wasn't based upon the memory of some grisly deeds performed in the Congo.

And I met more NGO people. A chubby, middle-aged UNICEF man from New Zealand was sitting with a younger, dark, and gloomy sidekick from Tajikistan. They worked with abandoned children who were often thrown in prison. If a child bride of thirteen or fourteen ran away from her arranged marriage, she was likely to wind up in jail, shunned by family and society.

I asked the guy from Tajikistan if he interacted well with the Afghan Tajiks. His response was a slight negative shrug. I'd heard that Soviet Muslim soldiers had returned to places like Tajikistan with grim stories about the Afghans. Did he believe these stories, I asked? This time his gesture was instant and affirmative. (The Tajik turned out to be an accountant.)

I overheard two earnest young British teachers, a man and a woman, loudly discussing their classroom teaching methods. The teachers belonged to a NGO and had come in a spirit of high idealism. Alas, their Afghan students displayed local quirks that totally thwarted the application of modern teaching college techniques. Unfortunately, the Brits didn't detail these quirks. The two rambled on morosely as I drank a Virgin Cola.

I woke early the next day to the sound of lustful donkeys and many cocks. Animals are never far away in large third world cities, unlike London or New York. And in many ways, Kabul is today like other over-crowded Asian cities. The dust is the same. The traffic is no worse. The insurgency doesn't intrude much. In Saigon in 1966, I had a constant sense of imminent danger. (The same as I felt once after blundering into East Cleveland.) In Kabul, I didn't feel that the locals had any specific interest in killing me.

Later, watching boys flying colorful kites in front of the Nadir Shah Mausoleum, perched high above the city, Kabul seemed much as it was in 1971. King Nadir Shah was assassinated in 1933. He had been put on the throne only a few years before that with the help of Waziris, Pashtun tribesmen from Waziristan in present-day Pakistan, just on the other side of the Durand Line, the arbitrary British-created border between Afghanistan and Pakistan. Waziristan is currently a main base of today's Taliban insurgents. Perhaps the Waziris will help change the Afghan regime again. Past, present, and future join up in Afghanistan.

Of course, other Asian cities don't have an American surveillance blimp tethered at three thousand feet over the city. Mr. Hassan and I watched the grey blimp as the boys flew their kites. The blimp had multiple cameras pointing downwards that presumably fed onto large screens covering the walls of some underground room in Colorado. Halfway up the cable tethering the blimp was a large Afghan flag. No doubt the blimp would please Tom Clancy, but I wondered about it. What would Americans feel if the French had a blimp tethered over Central Park? Would an American flag on the cable make us feel happier about it?

And in Kabul, as everywhere in Afghanistan, there are those maimed by war. Legless men on little wheeled carts, pushing themselves along with the flat of their hands. Or armless men sitting on the ground, begging with a bowl between their crossed legs.

Mr. Hassan told me that there had been a bomb at the Indian embassy while we were in the Panjshir Valley. This was undoubtedly linked to the Indo-Pakistani rivalry for influence in Afghanistan, and committed by local Pakistani proxies.

Kabul is ringed and divided by steep hills. We drove part way up the "TV Hill," from which Massoud's forces had randomly and pointlessly shelled Kabul not long ago. We walked the rest of the way to the top. Mr. Hassan stopped me when I started to leave the path, pointing out a small, red-painted rock that might, or might not, indicate the location of a mine.

Most mines were swept from within the city, but it was unwise to assume that none had been missed. We talked then of visiting the OMAR Land Mine Museum, but it was always closed. OMAR is the Organization for Mine Clearance and Afghan Rehabilitation. There all the horrors of mine warfare are on show.

I wanted to go up to the Bala Hisar, the ancient fortress which overlooks Kabul, but it is off limits as a military post.

We went on to Babur's Tomb, an exquisite work in white marble, surrounded by attractive gardens. In the gardens, a picnicking couple asked us to join them. This was the only place in Afghanistan that I saw girls and boys holding hands. The garden was full of Arghawan trees, also known as the Judas tree. These were covered with attractive seed pods. I took a few of the pods to find out if the tree could survive and bloom in the chilly climate of northwestern Connecticut. I had already gathered some rose hips from a wild rose growing over a Soviet tank, high in the Panjshir Valley.

Babur's Tomb is walled but open to the sky at his request. Babur conquered India and founded the Mogul Empire there but always preferred Kabul, which he conquered early in his career. He was a great man who wrote an autobiography that is said to be both interesting and of literary value. On Babur's headstone it is written that it was erected for "the light garden of the angel king." Shah Jehan, Babur's descendent, Mogul Emperor and creator of the Taj Mahal, built a lovely white marble mosque near the Tomb.

The whole tomb site is being beautifully restored by the Aga Khan Trust for Culture. The trust has erected a traditional brick caravanserai as a visitors center where there are shops selling Afghan handicrafts, including carpets that are made in the center by boy trainees.

I continued my questioning of Mr. Hassan. Land was bought and sold by the *jerib*. (For the curious, one *jerib* is twenty *biswas*.) A *jerib* equals an acre. To buy or sell land or property, you enter into a contract that is worded along the lines of "I, Hossein, the son of Ali, sell fifteen *jeribs* near Kandahar to Muhammad, the son of Hamid..."

There were other old local measures. Seven kilos, for example, equal one *sir*. Good to know these things.

On October 11, we left for Herat, for what would be my third visit.

Leaving the hotel at 4:30 a.m., we heard the muezzin calling the faithful for the first prayers of the day. It was necessary to leave early because of the elaborate security measures at the airport. We were searched three times—thoroughly—before entering the airport. After the last search, Mr. Hassan and I crowded onto an elderly bus that was to take us the two hundred yards to the terminal.

The bus arrived at the terminal, stopped, and the doors popped open. People started to exit when the bus lurched forward some twenty feet. In the United States, this would have caused screaming, followed by multiple real or imaginary injuries and a rush to find a good tort lawyer. The Afghans, men and women, young and old, simply hopped or jumped smartly off. Everyone landed safely on their feet.

Waiting for our plane, we could see a good selection of American attack helicopters, big old Russian helicopters, now painted white, with their long, drooping main rotor blades and last a solitary, massive Russian Antonov heavy lift aircraft.

The flight was again about the same comfort level as a typical United or Delta flight. But the mountain scenery from my window was more spectacular than anything I've seen in the United States or Europe. Raw, brown mountains, loose rocks, knife-sharp ridges— every square mile all points and sharp edges, ridge after ridge, with traces of new snow, and roadless valley after roadless valley, but foot paths and animal tracks everywhere—it was magnificent.

In Herat, we were picked up in a cherry red Toyota Camry by a louche young fellow of about twenty-five who looked Iranian. His dark hair was professionally cut, cropped close to his round head. He wore elegant black shoes. The car, on the other hand, had a worn and squeaking fan belt, and the seatbelts for the back seat were stuffed down under the seat. I made myself immediately unpopular by refusing to drive off until the belts were located and pulled out.

Mr. Hassan helpfully noted that all the fresh, recent graves in the Kabul British cemetery were inhabited by road accident victims, rather than war victims, but then made a show of not wearing a seat belt. Inshallah.

This louche driver, whom I won't name, was obviously an entrepreneur of sorts. The car was his. We soon stopped and picked up a friend of the driver's who said nothing then or later but somehow inserted himself into many of my photos. This other fellow rode shotgun.

The driver's real job was working for USAID, the US government aid agency. His role was in alternative agricultural development, though one look at his hands showed that he had never been anywhere near a spade. This did not matter. His US-taxpayer-financed work was in nearby Farah Province where the bad guys controlled much of the countryside. Going there at all was dangerous. Our driver only went there the number of times needed to satisfy his bosses at USAID.

The driver's USAID job was to offer advice to about one hundred farmers. He considered this fatuous. There were thousands of farmers; talking to a handful was pointless. If the farmers were to give up cultivating naughty plants like poppies, what they needed was credit to buy seeds and fertilizer and machinery. Advice was of little help. Growing poppies didn't require credit or machinery or much water or any fertilizer. Poppy buyers paid cash on the spot for the harvest.

The guy was hard not to dislike for his manner, but I was pretty sure that he was broadly telling the truth. If he was skimming something from USAID, he wasn't exactly alone. Every Toyota I saw proclaimed the extent of the corruption.

***

At least trying to aid Afghan farmers is not inherently silly or almost certain to be a complete waste of US taxpayer funds.

In thinking about the photo below, remember that most of the people in Afghanistan are illiterate, practically all are poor, and many are hungry. Remember also that most Afghan women have trouble leaving their houses on their own. The sign reads: Biodiversity Conservation in Afghanistan by Women. Note that it is a USAID project.

US Foreign Aid at Its Best, 2009

Everyone I talked with agreed that, if the American military left, our project teams and NGOs would soon follow. In some cases this would be a real loss, though useful international NGOs like the Aga Khan Foundation probably would remain, minus their US staff. Losing many of these US NGOs will be no true loss. Ultimately the Afghans have to sort out their own destiny, with or without the help of foreign "nation builders."

Herat had changed less than Kabul, though it too had been cruelly damaged in the civil wars. Country people had poured into the city as in Kabul. But it still had mature trees and familiar buildings, mosques and minarets. The weather was beautiful. But Herat and I got off somehow to an uneasy start.

For some reason, after dropping our stuff at the Five Star Hotel—yes, that was the name—we went to a nearby modern mausoleum constructed in the customary white marble. We parked and approached it over a scrubby, shit-and-garbage strewn field. The tomb was that of Mirwais Sadiq, who was assassinated in 2004. Sadiq was a government minister at the time but his only significance and the reason for his elaborate tomb was that Sadiq was a son of Ismail Khan, the warlord of Herat.

The career of Ismail Khan illustrates perfectly the difficulty faced by any elected leader of Afghanistan in dealing with powerful and undemocratic local leaders, who control not just gunmen but ethnic loyalties. These leaders may be financed independently of the central government through controlling loyal taxes and customs duties or by backhanders from foreign paymasters, or by both.

Herat was part of Persia until the 1700s. Geographically, all the east-west routes across Afghanistan pass through Herat. Naturally, the Iranians would like to control Herat by one means or other. The British fought a small, nasty war to prevent this in the nineteenth century.

At the time of the initial Communist takeover and government in Kabul, Ismail Khan was an officer in the Afghan National Army in Herat. He is a Dari, or Persian-speaking Tajik of powerful appearance and a majestic beard.

In early 1979, the garrison in Herat mutinied against the Communist governor of Herat in protest against arrests and assassinations of anti-Communists. The Kabul government promptly retaliated by having Soviet bombers annihilate Herat, killing thousands of people. Seizing the leadership, Ismail Khan slipped off into the countryside and formed a mujaheddin militia. Thus, he became a warlord.

Ismail Khan proved a shrewd and resilient commander. After his mujaheddin took Herat in 1992, he appointed himself governor. As the Taliban threat grew, Khan fought them in turn but with less success. When the previously mentioned General Dostum, the Uzbek leader from Mazar, switched sides, Dostum attacked Herat successfully. Ismail Khan fled into Iran with thousands of his men.

Just as the Afghan Pashtun Taliban are aligned with Pakistani Pashtun Taliban factions, Khan is assumed to be in the pocket of the Iranians.

Now, is that perfectly clear? Good, because the career of this remarkable scoundrel becomes really complicated after his return from Iran.

While organizing resistance to the Taliban, Khan was betrayed and captured by the Taliban. Held in Kandahar prison, Khan was then said to have "escaped" in March 1999. Since escaping from Taliban custody alive is rare, many believe that some foreign entity bought Khan's freedom in exchange for some unknown benefit.

Ismail Khan, however, gave at least the appearance of fighting against the Taliban after his "escape." For this, he was again formally made governor of Herat. By local accounts, Khan was a good governor in terms of rebuilding the city and encouraging commerce. He might even have won office in an open election. But his interests remained purely local and did not include passing on tax revenues to the new, American backed Afghan "Transitional Administration" government. This new and fragile central government, possibly urged on by the Americans, backed a rising in Herat by local military forces. Khan's son was killed during the brief uprising in muddled circumstances.

Whether son or father was the true object of the killing isn't clear. Afterwards, Khan suppressed the insurrection with little difficulty. Another failed assassination attempt on Khan was made on September 29, 2009. The Taliban claimed responsibility for this attempt. Ismail Khan plainly is lucky. To make sure that he remains lucky, Ismail Khan had the general who ordered his son's assassination blown up with a car bomb near the Salang Pass.

President Karzai recently tried to reappoint Ismail Khan to his new cabinet as energy minister, but the Afghan parliament vetoed the appointment. Since Khan won't go to Kabul for fear of yet another assassination attempt and has no known energy expertise, his role in the cabinet would have been titular.

The point of having Khan in the cabinet is to keep a lid on Herat. Think of the late Mayor Daley of Chicago, but a Daley with his own powerful private army. Even without an army, American presidents of whatever party found it expedient to pay court to Daley.

From an American governmental standpoint, getting men like Khan out of Afghan politics seems both moral and practical. Why, worthy Americans suggest, can't Karzai simply fill his cabinet with honest technocrats? As a mouthpiece of the US foreign policy establishment, the New York Times made this point in an editorial on January 9, 2010:

Lawmakers also wisely rejected the appointment of Ismail Khan as energy minister and three nominees associated with Gen. Abdul Rashid Dostum. Mr. Khan and General Dostum backed Mr. Karzai in the campaign. Both are notorious warlords accused of human rights abuses. If Mr. Karzai felt a debt to them, he should consider it repaid, distance himself from such unsavory cronies and reach out to other candidates.

Well, yes indeed.

But how will the ever-righteous New York Times rid us of the numerous "unsavory cronies" of our own senators and representatives? Anyway, President Karzai may have other priorities, since President Karzai presumably likes having his head attached to the top of his neck and perhaps takes a "think global, act local" approach to Afghan realities.

Thus, from a Washington DC perspective, in time it may prove convenient to get rid of Mr. Karzai, as various US establishment worthies have already proposed. After all, President Kennedy turned a blind eye to the murder of President Diem in Vietnam. And President Carter showed the Shah of Iran the meaning of "when push comes to shove." Puppet rulers can become more trouble than they are worth.

Back at the mausoleum, we talked with this splendid mujaheddin who was guarding the tomb.

Turbaned and of a certain age and dignity yet cheerful, this man had dyed his beard red. He was quite willing to be photographed but declined my suggestion that he in turn photograph me holding his well worn AK-47. Mr. Hassan said that finding jobs for aging ex-mujaheddin was a problem. These men had been through a lot and expected their leaders to look after them. In exchange, they were very loyal to these leaders, not to some notional government in Kabul or to the country called Afghanistan.

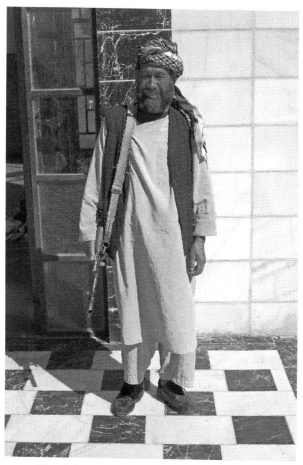

Ex-Mujaheddin Tomb Guard in Herat

For lunch, we went, as usual, to a kebab restaurant. I like Afghan kebabs, even through the small pieces of marinated beef or lamb are always interspersed with bits of fat that I don't eat. My technique is to grab the ring on the end of the skewer with one hand and pull off both meat and fat, and then, using scraps of bread held Afghan-style in my right hand, pick up and eat only the meat. I skip the raw vegetables like celery and tomatoes that are also served. It's not a balanced diet, but it's satisfactory for a middle-aged carnivore who hopes to avoid intestinal dramas.

This restaurant, the Argawan, was my first kebab disappointment. We sat on rugs on a raised platform under an overhang in the open air. Many, many flies jointed us. Pizza was on the menu, but perhaps unwisely I rejected this new addition to the Afghan diet and had my usual kebab. The bread was stale and the kebab lamb meat distinctly off. The bits of fat were rancid and smelled. I will not be going back to the Argawan.

Much of our time in Herat was spent visiting shrines and tombs. These were interesting in themselves, but of as much interest to me were the restored and new graveyards, usually in front of the shrine. The graves were marked by tall, elaborate white-marble gravestones, covered with verses from the Koran in Arabic script. Mr. Hassan said that one of the first results of aid money leaking into the economy through corruption was a keen desire to upgrade a family's graves.

Traditionally, a Muslim grave in Afghanistan was a stark affair on a hillside. The grave was shallow, resulting in a raised mound. Loose stones covered the raised mound. If the person buried was a martyr for Islam or person of Islamic virtue, a green triangular banner on a plain wooden stick would flutter in the wind over the grave. I found these puritanical, austere graveyards as moving as those in New England. The updated ones seemed garish in comparison.

As we wandered through the shrines, Mr. Hassan told me about Afghan funeral customs. The body of the newly dead was taken away by the local mullahs who washed it three times with special oils. Then they wrapped the body in three separate white cloths.

As with Jews, the burial must take place within a short time after death. The grave is prepared and the body placed in it upon the body's right side, facing Mecca. Then the grave is filled in with flat stones and mud put in the cracks between the stones. Finally, soil is added to top up the grave. As the mourners pass the grave, they use a little shovel to throw more soil on the grave.

At the first prayer at 4:30 a.m. on the day following the internment, the family gathers at the grave to say prayers. Later, there is a two-hour commemorative service at the mosque. Families are not necessarily buried together. The wishes of the deceased are generally respected if, for example, a family member wishes to be buried in his ancestral village.

◆

The Five Star Hotel is a large, modern, cement stump like an airport Sheraton with multiple levels of security to go through before checking in. On the street, there were guards and a barricade. Up a short drive, we passed through a high wall. Inside the wall, steel blast gates were pulled back for the day. A green Ford pickup truck with a new American machine gun on a raised mount was parked just inside the wall. Afghan police were hanging around the truck.

To enter the glass-fronted lobby, we passed through a metal detector, watched by a doorman with an AK-47. As we checked in, music from *The Phantom of the Opera* was playing loudly in the background. There were few other guests, it appeared. We ate dinner in a large, mostly empty room. Though unappealing to look at, the buffet did not make me sick. Plus, the service was endearingly friendly. All restaurant service in Afghanistan is done by men.

The Five Star Hotel had standards. The wool sweater I left on a chair in my room was taken away, washed, and dried on what must have been the hottest setting on the dryer. When I found the clean sweater neatly folded on the bed in the evening, it would have fitted a six-year-old perfectly.

One thing, though, about this hotel made me uneasy. And it wasn't just the fact that the hotel towels smelled strongly of lamb fat. The hotel building was on a bare hillside off a fairly busy road. There is no cover in any direction. Ramming a truck with a suicide bomb into the back wall would have been easy. Would the guards have fought back in an attack? I wandered up and down the corridor outside my room, thinking about places to hide. There weren't any. However, I slept well.

After my trip, the US Government leased the Five Star Hotel as the site of the future US consulate in Herat. Predictably, the hotel was attacked with a rocket-propelled grenade shortly afterwards in January 2010. There were no casualties, but the building will always be an obvious, easy target and hence an odd choice for a consulate. No doubt the surrounding walls will be increased in height and thickened.

Next morning, we went first to the tomb of a grandson of the sixth Shia Imam. Remember that there are twelve Imams, or God-chosen spiritual leaders, in the Shia theology. Most came to sticky ends. The twelfth Imam simply vanished. Shias believe that the twelfth is the Mahdi, or savior, who will return to rule in glory, a sort of equivalent to the Christian belief in a second coming. For now, the Mahdi is in occultation, alive but not revealed.

Anyone related to the twelve original Imams has a patina of holiness. This particular Imam's grandson was murdered. His killer was executed, but the killer's body would not stay in the grave (apparently it popped out of the ground) until the murderer was finally buried at the feet of the murdered grandson.

Traditionally, pious Muslim pilgrims walk counterclockwise around a tomb like this one while praying. However, the Taliban do not approve of such idolatry. So a glass barrier was erected to block this pilgrimage circulation around the tomb, which is typical of the petty meanness of the Taliban. There are no cinemas in Herat because the Taliban wrecked or closed them.

Outside, in front of the tomb, an elderly scholar explained some beautiful Kufic inscriptions for us.

The next day we visited the most remarkable historic sites of Herat. First, we went to the local outpost of the Ministry of Culture to obtain a permit to visit Herat Castle, whose massive bulk I remembered well. The culture director was away from his desk, and the time of his return could not be predicted. We hung around for a while before going to the Musalla complex.

The Musalla complex, though largely in ruins, remains one of the most important examples of Islamic art and architecture in the world. What we see today is a ruined fraction of what once was on the site, and yet it is still startlingly impressive and beautiful.

To understand the full artistic and cultural significance of the site and the disasters that ruined it, read Robert Byron's masterpiece, *The Road to Oxiana*. This book remains an essential guide for understanding the artistic heritage of Iran and Afghanistan.

We went first to the Tomb of Gowhar Shad, a most remarkable woman, who was the wife of Shah Rukh, the son of Timur the Lame or Tamerlane. She was as great a patron of the arts as Catherine di Medici. There were birds chirping and children playing in front of the Tomb. There was also a very aggressive dog that I managed to face down, to the great relief of Mr. Hassan. Eye contact and a loud voice are usually enough to overawe even an Afghan dog, but have a stone in your hand just in case.

Around the tomb site stand a number of remarkable blue-tiled minarets. Five minarets remain out of the original twenty. One, near the entrance to the complex, has a great hole in it from a Soviet shell and stands at an unnatural angle, held up by steel cables.

At the back of the complex are the remains of another minaret, destroyed by Soviet artillery. Perhaps Allah was displeased by this moronic act of destruction. A burned-out, wrecked Soviet self-propelled howitzer is permanently lodged below the ruins of the minaret the howitzer may have destroyed.

Souvenir of Russia: Herat, 2009

Behind the howitzer, land has been cleared for the construction of new corruption-financed Afghan-style McMansions, complete with one-way mirror glass. Not all the destruction in Afghanistan is due to foreigners.

I picked up a small, rectangular piece of turquoise-blue glazed tile from this ruin. This piece of tile, like the minaret, dates from the early 1400s. It now sits on my desk.

The Musalla complex was surprisingly intact until 1885 when, like the Summer Palace in Beijing, it became a casualty of imperial overreach. The British were expecting an invasion of Herat by the Russians, who had massed troops to the north. So, British military engineers blew up much of the complex to establish fields of fire for their artillery.

Since the Russians never got around to invading Afghanistan until the Soviets arrived, the British act of vandalism was pointless. And prior to the Soviets, twentieth-century earthquakes destroyed two more minarets. Now, the extremely busy truck route that runs past the complex is likely to cause several more minarets to collapse through vibration.

The only bright spot is that the Aga Khan Foundation is financing the restoration of the Gowhar Shad Tomb, which already looks splendid under its new turquoise dome.

We went on to the Friday Mosque, the main mosque of Herat. Not only is this a truly majestic building, we had it to ourselves. There was not another soul to be seen. There is much to be said for being a tourist in a war zone.

No religion appeals to me on a rational level, but ancient mosques, like this masterpiece, move me. Dating from 1200 AD, this is one of the world's great religious buildings.

We wandered into the tile workshop of the Mosque. There, craftsmen work in the same way as their ancestors. Square or rectangular tiles are fired and then glazed with the same colors used a thousand years ago. Workers sitting cross legged on rugs take the colored tiles and fashion then into the right sized pieces to fit into the intricate patterns of the Mosque exterior. The pieces of tile are assembled and fixed onto a large frame or backing which is then actually hung like a painting on the Mosque exterior.

The head of the workshop was delighted to chat with us. He said he had worked on tiles for forty years. His face and manner became animated when he told us that to his joy one of his sons has followed him in the trade and that we had seen the son working on the dome of the Gowhar Shad Tomb. There is hope for these monuments if such craftsmen are given the time and money they need to restore them.

Master Tile Worker: Friday Mosque, Herat, 2009

Appropriately, we went from the Friday Mosque to the row of antique shops outside the main entrance of the Mosque. One of the shops, Sultan Hamidy's, is attached to a tiny glassworks where a solitary glass-blower makes objects out of the blue glass for which Herat is famous.

The glass blower is a hunchback who earns ten dollars a day. His kiln is fired by wood, and another man works constantly to keep the fire hot enough.

Glass Blower—Herat 2009

We went back to Sultan Hamidy's shop. The Sultan himself showed us through his remarkable stock which included Greek coins, glass objects old and new, and an infinite range of Afghan jewelry: earrings, bangles, hair ornaments, and others of obscure use. Many were decorated with lapis lazuli, of which Afghanistan is the world's main source. Some were silver. Anyone, male or female, would enjoy spending hours in this mad jumble of a shop. Which, again, we had to ourselves.

Finally, we went back to get our permit to visit Herat Castle. The representative of the culture ministry was at last present and delighted to have a bona fide tourist visit Herat. After visiting the castle, we agreed to meet him again at a US-sponsored photo exhibit.

Herat Castle, or the Citadel of Ikhtiar-ad-Din, is a massive fourteenth-century structure whose size and image of power reflect the importance of Herat as the western control point for entering Afghanistan. On a vast scale like a crusader castle, it is perfectly described by Robert Byron in great detail. Think of massive walls, loopholes, and many turrets.

Like Robert Byron, we had a soldier attached to us as we scrambled up the different levels of the castle. The castle is being superbly restored but currently lacks such tourist amenities as handrails on the many stone steps or anything to stop the idiotic from falling over the edge of the battlements. This is not a place for vertigo sufferers.

Unlike Robert Byron, we had no trouble with our military guide. Byron, a feisty descendent of the poet, had trouble with most of the people he encountered. Our soldier was a charming fellow who took us back to the guardhouse and gave us tea. He was a literate man of about forty who had been in heavy fighting during the civil wars. Now, though sick of soldiering, he only has his tiny army paycheck to support a large family. He spends his abundant free time reading. His literacy was unusual and made me wonder what his past was and how the wars had warped his life.

A younger soldier was also in the guardhouse, lying on a wooden bunk. He too was very friendly but distracted by a daytime TV program that he was watching on an ancient black-and-white TV with a rabbit ear antenna. The plot of the Bollywood-style program was so obvious—family turmoil due to marital problems—that Mr. Hassan and I watched it happily for a while despite the shaky picture and my inability to understand a word of the dialogue.

In Afghanistan, TV has taken the place of going to movies and is highly popular but controversial. The most popular program on private TV *Today* is suspected of Jewish input because women sometimes appear on it in more-or-less Western clothes, totally devoid of head-to-floor tenting.

The photograph exhibition was in the ancient main cistern of Herat, next to the castle. With the water long drained away, the huge, domed tank is perfect for exhibitions. It is delightfully cool inside.

The photos were by Steve McCurry, famous for his *National Geographic* cover of the Afghan refugee girl. The exhibition is called *In the Shadow of the Mountains.* McCurry is a gifted photographer who has a special feel for Afghans. He even managed to photograph unveiled Afghan women and girls, something I failed to do, even with the offer of a petty bribe.

Our Soldier Guide at Herat Castle

Our new pal, the representative of the culture ministry, was there to greet us, along with Brad Hansen, a US diplomat, who is to be the American consul when the Herat consulate is opened. Hansen was dressed for a Princeton history department faculty meeting circa 1973: blue blazer, grey flannels, and striped tie. Though I am pretty sure that I was the only American tourist in Herat, Hansen was obviously displeased to see me. For some reason, I was the turd in his punch bowl. I couldn't be bothered to find out why.

Perhaps Hansen feared that I was secretly a US politician or, even worse, someone sent to check on his expenses. Hansen appeared to be in his early sixties, a few years younger than I am. I tried to learn what he was doing but only found out that decades ago he had learned Persian in the Peace Corps in Iran. I don't want to suggest that Hansen was nasty; just cold and off-hand. Possibly something he ate.

Early the next morning, Mr. Hassan and I were driven out to the airport by our louche USAID driver. Along the way, he pointed out a business park that had been shut down by threats of kidnapping the owner-managers. There had indeed been many kidnappings, some fifty in Herat during the recently ended Ramadan.

One of these businessmen, a cousin of our USAID guy, had been kidnapped and ransomed for a hundred thousand dollars.

"The kidnappers were policemen," he said.

"You mean that they were dressed as policemen?" I said.

"No, I mean that they were policemen."

The driver is planning to move to the UK shortly. I wished him luck.

Herat Airport was full of passengers waiting for the security office to open. The airport waiting area is open air and surrounded by a high wall. There is one small waiting room for women and a few scattered benches, mostly not placed in what little shade exists. I was in a cheerful mood, despite having had the wheels of my bag finally come off, defeated like so many foreigners by the Afghan terrain.

It was good that I was in this mood, because it soon became clear that something wasn't working as normal. I milled around, talking to people. Everyone talks freely to perfect strangers in Afghanistan. Since there was no notice board or announcements in any form, theories abounded as to why the planes were neither landing nor taking off. A surprising number of people spoke English. And, as the hours drifted by, I talked to most of them.

Mr. Mehdi, an Iranian oil and gas merchant, told me loudly that he loved the Afghan people so much that he wanted Herat to be part of Iran again. The small group around us seemed to think that this was a perfectly acceptable sentiment; Mr. Hassan, however, was disgusted and said equally loudly that he was glad not to have to have business dealings with Mr. Mehdi or with Iranians in general. Mr. Mehdi responded that he considered the rule of the Ayatollahs in Iran to be part of a British plot to discredit Iran and that Iran was much misunderstood. Crazy theories about the British are alive and well in Iran just as they were in 1971, and just as they will be in 2071. Crazy will always play well in Iran.

A young and upbeat Afghan guy in a Western suit told me that he was flying via Dubai to Zambia. He and his brother-in-law were going to buy precious stones there and sell them via a cousin in New York City.

My most interesting contact was a young man who was Afghan but had been taken by his refugee parents to Holland as a baby. He spoke fluent English with a slight Dutch accent. The young man's parents had been idealistic Communist intellectuals involved with Kabul University. He said that Communist rule had been honest and only Communist in name; there had been no effort to collectivize agriculture or to seize lawful property. It was a tragedy that foreign intervention ruined this experiment. The Afghans paid a terrible price for their role in the ending of the Cold War and lost their best chance of becoming modern and secular. Not knowing in detail what the Communists had done or not done during their brief rule, I could only nod as the young guy spoke. Becoming "modern and secular" didn't relate well to what I knew of Afghan needs and desires, though.

By this time it was hot. The sun was full overhead. The morale of the waiting, would-be passengers was slipping. We were distracted by a scuffle at the main gate into the airport. A man in traditional garb was grappling with a young, vigorous woman who was wearing a police uniform. The woman was trying to get away from the man and retreat into a metal shipping container used as a police office. A middle-aged male police officer stood by the wrestling pair, shouting at them but not intervening.

Mr. Hassan pieced together what was happening. The woman was the fiancée of the man who was pulling at her. He wished her to come away with him. She wished to complete her police duty because she liked getting paid, and her parents needed the money. Mr. Hassan said that her wishes were irrelevant; she belonged to her fiancée, and her police job was over, effective now.

No one did anything. Mr. Hassan was horribly embarrassed. "This is the Afghan way," he said. "By tradition, the man is right." But Mr. Hassan, a kind man with three much-loved daughters, did not approve. However, in public it would be highly dangerous to intervene. The young policewoman, now subdued, went away with her violent fiancé.

While this was going on, a large boy never stopped throwing sizable stones at a smaller boy. No one did anything about that either, including cowardly me. Time hung on our hands. People discussed the various regional airlines. The newly formed private ones were alright, it seemed. But Ariana, the Afghan national airline, was downright dangerous and known as "Scariana."

The worst, though, everyone agreed was Pakistan International Airlines, or PIA. It had too many nicknames to remember, but here is a sample:

Parachute Is Advised,
Perhaps I Arrive,
and *Please Inform Allah.*

In such simple ways, we chatted away the time. It was now early afternoon. Luckily, we then had a wonderful military spectacle to divert us. Herat Airport is only a kilometer or so from a major NATO base. We first heard the noise of helicopters, and then watched five or six military helicopters swoop fast over the airport. Some were troop carriers; two were helicopter gunships. We could follow the helicopters as they headed off across the flat terrain to some point to the right of Herat. Pretty soon after that, a good deal of black smoke appeared on the horizon, but we were too far away to hear anything.

At the same time, there was much vehicle noise out on the main road in front of the airport. I managed to get up on the roof of a low shed inside the perimeter wall. A convoy of Italian armored personnel carriers was going by, with Italian soldiers in berets and wraparound reflective sunglasses manning the machine guns on top.

Your Taxpayer Dollars at Work—Herat 2009

Several Afghan men climbed up on the roof with me to watch. With gestures, they indicated to me that it was forbidden to take photos, but when a line of American MRAPs came by, I could not resist. The MRAP is a massive, and massively expensive, mine resistant armored personnel carrier. This one I photographed appears to belong to the US Navy, a mere thousand or so miles from the nearest open water.

In the middle of this excitement, Mr. Hassan learned somehow that all flights were cancelled because of the military activity. A town not far from Herat was the objective of the helicopter assault. This town was the home base of the former mayor of Herat, who had been fired by the government. In a sulk, he retreated to his hometown along with his small private army. There the ex-mayor instigated a kidnap ring and built a private prison for his captives.

Later that afternoon, we were told that NATO troops seized the town, killed the ex-mayor, and captured his son-in-law who was second in command. The prisoners were freed. Everyone knew about the venal, dangerous mayor. His behavior was what Afghans expected. One man recited:

Jaye Ke Palaw As,
Sharwal Ba Jelow As.

This was translated as:

Wherever there is food,
First there will be the mayor.

Finally, we gave up and went back to the Five Star Hotel.

———◆———

The next day we managed to fly back to Kabul, but we arrived too late for me to fly out of Afghanistan. I spent the night in the Gandamack Lodge, which is operated by an Englishman. The Lodge is thought to have the best security in Kabul, but I couldn't see why this is so. It is just a jumble of buildings up a narrow lane. No blast wall. No mirrors on long rods to look under the cars. Perhaps the Englishman is particularly skillful in buying off possible threats or just lucky.

The rooms at the Gandamack Lodge are decorated in somewhat the style of an English country house with hunting prints on the walls. That, plus the 580 channels available on the room TV, caused me to have a severe bout of cognitive dissonance. Most of the channels featured mullahs from every known Islamic society holding forth on what I assumed were Koranic topics.

Early the next morning, Mr. Hassan and the driver took me out to the airport. The security was intense. I thanked Mr. Hassan profusely. He is a wonderful guide. We are still in touch. I would love to make another trip with him.

The flight back to the United States was uneventful. The transit lounge of Delhi Airport was lively this time because I shared it with the Junior National Football Team of Tajikistan. The boys were spirited when they were not aggressively praying on rugs they had brought with them. Their coach sported a fine, traditional set of Russian-style stainless steel front teeth. True, the boys spat on the floor from time to time as European players like David Beckham do. But they were nice boys. They had just beaten Nepal in Katmandu and were looking forward to playing in the Asia Cup.

During the long flight back, I thought hard about poor, beautiful, broken Afghanistan. Theories abound as to whether or not the American military effort will succeed or whether Pakistan will continue to cooperate. The media will provide encouraging reports of important Taliban leaders being killed or of vital towns (consisting of a crossroads, some mud-walled buildings, and a few terrified goats) being liberated. US politicians with blow-dried hair will hold forth about military strategy and demand an immediate end to whatever they think is happening or not happening.

All of this is so much kerfuffle. The Taliban have a wonderful saying, "You have the watches; we have the time." The Taliban are mostly Pashtuns and represent a major ongoing theme within Pashtun society. The Pashtun are some 40 per cent of the Afghan population. The Taliban won't go away. And major parts of Pakistan will remain Pashtun dominated.

Consider the map below showing the Pashtun tribal areas in Afghanistan and Pakistan. Notice that the border is more-or-less irrelevant to these free-moving tribesmen. The border, after all, is a British invention and totally arbitrary. The ethnic distribution of the Pashtuns shows why they have often dreamed of "Pushtunistan," their own country with more logical borders. The map also shows why Pakistan is a key part of the Taliban problem.

Eventually, the Afghans themselves will have to sit down together as they have many times in the past and hold a loya jirga. The different factions, tribes, and ethnic groups will shape some kind of messy truce. American officials may play some role in this process, but it is only likely to be fully completed after the American soldiers leave. Whether the results of this loya jirga will turn out to have been worth the life of a single American soldier can be left for future historians to decide. To find out, though, first we have to leave.

Leave now, America!

Part of the American problem is that most Americans at home and even those in Afghanistan today have no idea of what Afghanistan was like not that long ago. Nor can they imagine the joy of travelling in a leisurely and erratic manner by road across Asia—and not in a MRAP.

Fate was kind to Alyson and me. We were lucky enough to find love and to travel in a way that may never again be possible. Still, decent people must hope that, despite all the political obstacles facing them, the Afghans find some sort of peace.

And perhaps, just perhaps, before we are hopelessly decrepit, Alyson and I will travel again together in wonderful Afghanistan.

Made in the USA
Middletown, DE
27 May 2019